"If you long for a re
transparent, satisfyi
With vulnerable openness and gut-level honesty, Tanya
Glanzman reveals her journey from brokenness to beauty,
from unwanted to daughter of the Most High God. Her il-
lustrations are riveting, but the biblical content that flows
from each chapter will heal your heart, encourage your
faith, and give you a platform upon which you can give
hope to others. This book has my highest recommenda-
tion—for personal and for small group use. Questions are
included for discussion and journaling. Read this important book yourself and buy more copies to give away. It will
transform your life."

CAROL KENT

Speaker and Author
He Holds My Hand: Experiencing God's Presence and Protection (*Tyndale*)

"From the strongest to the weakest, every woman needs
to hear what this book is saying. All of us have been hurt.
No matter where you are in your healing process, the
message in this book is an intentional but delicately ap-
plied cleansing, balm, and bandage. From Tanya's personal story to her profound pointing to the Truth, *My
Father's Daughter* has undoubtedly become a manual, a
guide, a reminder on my journey of healing. It will be for
my daughters as well."

JUDY MARTIN HESS

"How do we learn to trust our heavenly father–God–when human parents have hurt us deeply through neglect, abuse, or absence? Author and counselor Tanya Glanzman has spent a lifetime moving forward to embrace healing and hope which she shares generously in her new book, *My Father's Daughter*. Every daughter will glean fundamental principles of learning to live as God's beloved, finding healthy identity in Christ, and discerning voices of truth versus the world's noise of comparison and shame. *"God knew what I needed... I had to choose to face the years of woundedness, rejection, abuse, and abandonment that I had been the entirety of my adult life trying to forget."* Personal stories woven with solid biblical teaching make this a valuable, life-giving resource for anyone willing (or desperate) to find purpose in your pain."

LUCINDA SECREST McDOWEL

Author
Life-Giving Choices, Soul Strong

"Do you wonder who really loves you? Do you long for a Daddy who wraps his arms around you? Do you know who you belong to that will never leave you, hurt you, or betray you? If you can't answer those questions, you need the words on these pages. They'll change your life today."

JILL SAVAGE

Author
Real Moms... Real Jesus

"Many years ago, I had the privilege to meet Tanya. We became instant friends. Kindred sisters trudging through a heap of dysfunction and searching to know–really know–the love of God. As the years go by, we cross paths, laugh together, cry together and I learned quickly. She knows! She knows the intimate relationship with God that became the catalyst of knowing herself and knowing SHE is loved. And now, written here, YOU and I can follow along and learn these things together. Here, you will KNOW you are loved."

CHONDA PIERCE

Comedian
www.chonda.org

"Tanya's counseling degree allows her to address difficult and deep issues with wisdom and grace, but most importantly, her intimate relationship with Christ enables her to point those who are wounded to freedom. In *My Father's Daughter*, Tanya writes with authenticity and transparency, balancing powerful truths in Scripture with personal stories."

JENNIFER SLATTERY

Author and Speaker, Founder of *Wholly Loved Ministries*
Restoring Her Faith, Hometown Healing, Healing Love, Restoring Love,
Breaking Free, Intertwined, When Dawn Breaks, Beyond I Do

Printed in the United States of America

First Printing, 2020

ISBN 978-1-946389-18-3

STORY. PRESERVED.

2106 Main Street / PO Box 201 / Winesburg, OH 44690

www.jpvpress.com

For my Abba Father
who has loved me in my good, my bad, and my ugly,
and has called me His own.

Contents

SECTION ONE
You Are Loved

SECTION TWO
You Are Forgiven

SECTION THREE
You Are Chosen

SECTION FOUR
You Are Seen

SECTION FIVE
You Are Led

SECTION SIX
You Are Supplied

ACKNOWLEDGMENTS

I'm thankful to my King who placed this book in my heart long ago and has helped it come to fruition at just the right time.

My Beloved, Luke, for always believing in the Him in me so that this lighthouse can shine bright.

My sweet sister Amy, we both know that this (and so many other things) would never have happened without you. Thank you... with my whole heart.

Brooke and Tyler, thank you for your encouragement and patience as I've given so much time and attention to this project and my calling. Brooke, your editing skills are a gift to me!

Mom and Dad, thank you for always cheering me on and being proud of me.

Lolly-Mom, for your endless encouragement... thank you.

Mama Carol, for always believing this was possible and encouraging me to never stop saying "yes" to Him, no matter what.

Beth, thank you for never being surprised, quoting that discipline verse to me one million times, and teaching me to be thankful... always.

Lisa, for investing in me in so many ways... thank you.

Cammie, Charles, and every other person who has prayed for me and shined His love into my life by seeing through the trash to the treasure within, even from the beginning... thank you.

And finally, to Sue, Phil, and JPV Press for this amazing opportunity and for working so graciously with me to help share these truths with the world... thank you.

You are fully known, fully seen, and fully loved. It's been that way always.

Your worth and value... they are beyond measure. And you have a Father who delights in you.

He is a good, kind, and loving Father. He's not mad. He's not frustrated. He's not disappointed.

Your entire life, He has been waiting to hold you close. To be invited by you to take part in your life.

His heart longs to heal every wounded place in your soul. In fact, He's the only one who can.

So if you're tired, worn out, and weary, exhausted from trying to figure out this life on your own, I invite you to invite Him into your life. He has been excitedly waiting for this very moment. Like a joy-filled new Father,

His heart swells with love for you. Run, Daughter. Run full speed into the arms that have been waiting to hold you and begin living in the peace, healing, and joy for which you were created. It's simply a decision to accept the gift that has been offered to you. The gift of being loved the way you were created to be.

If this is a decision you have made and would like to find out more, please reach out and let me know; I would love to pray with you and welcome you into the family!

- *My Father's Daughter*

Introduction

After years of working with women, I am fully convinced that contentment is not due to the circumstances that surround us but because of what happens within us. There is no question; challenging times will come for all of us in different seasons. Although the face of the difficulties may change, the results end up being the same:

~ Low self-esteem

~ Anxiety

~ Shame

~ Insecurity

~ Guilt

~ Depression

~ Stress

~ Condemnation

~ Rejection

~ Abandonment

I daily encounter each of these issues—and many more—within both my ministry and inside the four walls of my counseling office. Every woman I spend time with is looking for something more, something different, something better.

Each obstacle offers the opportunity to overcome or be overcome, to sink or swim.

These women's hearts are longing for the answers they need to arrive at the destination of peace and—if it's not too much to ask for—joy. Hopelessness abounds as they admit they have done everything they know to do and yet have come up short.

At times, the most grueling battles we face come not from outside sources but from within. "I'm my own worst enemy," I've heard time and time again. "I'm harder on myself than anyone else is on me."

> *"I know that God's Word says that He loves, He forgives, etc., and I can believe that about others, but I just can't believe it applies to me."*

This type of belief system tells me that somewhere along the way, someone lied to them.

"I know that God's Word says that He loves, He forgives, etc., and I can believe that about others, but I just can't believe it applies to me."

What we believe about God and what we believe He believes about us are not only important, but are crucial to our overall mental, emotional, and spiritual well-being.

This is where the importance of identity comes in. The importance of knowing who we are and Whose we are. The importance of knowing beyond a shadow of a doubt that we are loved, treasured, and even adored by the One whose opinion matters most. When we can fully perceive and know what it means to be a daughter of the King, we are able to find the strength and courage to rise above any circumstance we face, reflecting to the world both the joy and the peace that Christ died for us to have. In the midst of difficult times, we will be able to say, "It is well with my soul," and really mean it.

You are your Father's Daughter. He is madly, deeply, and irrevocably in love with you. It won't change. It can't change. It's a done deal.

The more we rest in this knowledge and truth, the more capable we are of facing each challenge this life offers with both courage and faith.

Have you ever played that "getting to know you" game where someone asks, "If you had just one superpower, what would you choose?" Seldom has a question been simpler for me to answer. If I had one superpower, just one, this is what I would hope for: that I could open the heart of each woman I encounter and pour into her the knowledge of God's unfathomable love for her. That I could open her eyes and help her to see herself the way God sees her. That I could fully convince her that NO MATTER where she has come from, what she has done, or who she has been, she has a heavenly Father who is madly and deeply in love with her and who longs to spend each moment of her life being the source of everything she needs. There is no truth more vital.

This knowledge is the key to the FREEDOM, PEACE, and JOY that every woman needs.

He likes you, AND He loves you. You are His Beloved.

SECTION ONE
You Are Loved

> *We love Him because He first loved us.*
>
> 1 JOHN 4:19

Chapter One

> *Perfect love casts out fear.*
> 1 JOHN 4:18

Have you ever run across a talk show featuring an episode on parent/child reunions? The audience, after hearing the story of the individuals who will be reunited, is offered a front-row seat to the first encounter of two people who had, for assorted reasons, been separated from one another. Everyone claps through their tears, the host wraps up the episode with a huge smile and a fond farewell, the climatic music decrescendos, and everyone goes home.

The guests who were the focus of the show are now left face-to-face and heart-to-heart with someone who they were intended to have had relationship with all along. This causes them to feel close on one level, and yet they must now walk through the motions of establishing elements of true relationship and, perhaps eventually, emotional intimacy. The heart's longing for that which "should have been," mixed with the reality that relationships are not "built in a day," must make for an interesting journey. I've often wondered how those two individuals proceed after the excitement of the reunite.

Although I remember always believing in God, it wasn't until I was twenty-one that my heart was eternally united with Him. The initial days of my salvation were much like the excitement, music, and lights of one of those popular television talk shows. The weight of a single decision had impacted my entire life. In a moment, I went from...

condemned to saved,

guilty to forgiven,

tainted to pure,

victim to overcomer.

Never again would I know what it was to be alone or unloved.

That God-shaped hole within me was experiencing the first taste of what had always been intended to fill it. It was at this point that I realized the insufficiency of previous substitutes. The introduction to my Savior was glorious, and I reveled in...

His peace that transcended my understanding,

His joy that was my strength,

His mercy that was new every morning,

His love that held no limits.

It was a glorious time.

And yet, life goes on. The warm embrace of New Birth held firm, but the reality of life quickly came back into view. Venturing forward into the everyday, I was now face-to-face and heart-to-heart with a Savior whom I did not know. As I was mentored in truth, I quickly learned that this relationship required more than just the acceptance of my Savior; it required the offering of my heart to my Father. Trust, faith, and obedience were key, and this is where I struggled.

I had never known a Father's love. Those things that we all associate with having a father—daddy/daughter dances, strong arms to rescue you, protection, safety, unconditional love and affirmation—none of these were part of my personal experience. From age two to fourteen, each man that entered my life took his turn as a thief, stealing from me sacred things that were never meant for him. Sexual, emotional, and physical abuse characterized my relationship with anyone I had ever called "Father." Control, manipulation, and fear summarized my experiences with those whom I had called "Dad." My life's evidence connected the word "Daddy" with pain, fear, and mistrust. I'd never known a father that was good. I'm not sure I believed that those two words could ever be synonymous.

For a very long time, my way of loving the Father was simply to allow Him to love me. Like an overtired infant that has nothing to give, it was a good day when I could rest and trust enough to allow Him to hold me, receiving the comfort He offered, rather than flailing about in life, consumed by my own misery. Each time I was willing to become vulnerable enough to spend time in His presence, seek His face, and hear His voice, He was abundantly faithful, gentle, and patient, leading me ever so slowly into those deeper places of intimacy with Him.

After years of relationship, trust came more easily. He taught me through everyday life that He could be trusted. Patiently, He guided me into a deeper relationship with Him. Mercifully, He answered every question, fear, and doubt. He was faithful to continue the good work that He began within me, binding up my broken heart and making every place whole.

Over time, the scales of mistrust and suspicion fell from my eyes, helping me see my Father clearly. As with most relationships, it was our time spent together that made the difference.

As I spent time with Him, sitting quietly, ingesting and meditating upon His Word, I came to know His character and His heart for me. The more I got to know HIM, the easier it became to distinguish His voice from the voice I had been familiar with for so long. The voice that had always told me I was trash, worthless, and unlovable was drowned out by the sweet whispers of the one that called me His own.

Cherished

Loved

Treasured

"Perfect love casts out fear" (1 John 4:18). Really, it does. The more I learned, through His Word, the truth of how very much He loved me, the freer I was to love Him. The light of who He was shone through, revealing that He was the safe place for which I had always longed. Now free to love Him, we grew closer at an accelerated pace. I learned that only I determined the limits on how close we could become; He would never tire of spending time with me, hearing my heart, and rejoicing over me with singing (Zephaniah 3:17).

Chapter Two

> *We love Him because He first loved us.*
> 1 JOHN 4:19

This verse conjures up remembrances of myself many months pregnant, rubbing my belly while singing the first lullabies my first-born would ever hear. I loved her. I hadn't seen her. I hadn't known her. But even before I knew her, I knew her. I had never seen her face, and yet I would have died for her. She was mine. I revel in the fact that at that point, she had not done one thing to make me happy or proud of her. I loved her simply because she existed, and she belonged to me.

Similarly, our Heavenly Father doesn't love us because we are "good." We can never be good enough to be worthy of His love. He has deemed us worthy through Christ's death upon the cross and our acceptance of His sacrifice. He doesn't love us because we read our Bible, pray, or serve in the church nursery. It's not the Wednesday night Bible study or the early morning devotion we checked off. It's not our level of faith or how well we've kept our patience or held our tongue with our child, spouse, or coworker. No, beloved, He loves us because He is love. He can't help but love. It's all that He is—nothing more, nothing less. This is truth that should make our hearts rejoice.

Think on this, Daughter of the King: If God's love were dependent upon our actions when we are "good," then it would also waver when we are "not-so-good." When I consider my ratio of good to not-so-good, I am thankful that, unlike me, God is the same all the time (Hebrews 13:8). He never changes, never falters, and never has a bad day. He is stable and fixed in His love for us, and rather than being dependent upon our behavior, His love rests solely upon the gracious gift of our salvation through Jesus Christ, His Son. It is His answer to every place He knew we would fail to be worthy of the amazing, awe-inspiring love He longed to lavish upon us.

> There is no fear in love; but perfect love casts
> out fear, because fear involves torment. But he
> who fears has not been made perfect in love.
> (1 John 4:18)

Fear and torment join ranks to ravage the hearts of many daughters of the King. With tears streaming down their faces, they share with me the anguish in their hearts. I hear this from women who say they have known the Lord their entire lives, and from those who only contemplate what it might be like to know Him. They experience the fear of not being good enough, of messing up, of being rejected, abandoned—of missing the mark one too many times. Tormenting fear is paralyzing and is a tool of the enemy to cause every daughter of God to get stuck in her tracks.

How do we get here? Why is there such a struggle to believe that the God we love and serve could just as well love us? So often I've heard it said, "I know what the Bible says is true, and I am able to believe it about other people, but I just can't believe that it could apply to me."

The message we have been given through others often solidifies our inability to believe that we could be...

fully seen,

fully known,

fully loved.

These are lies the enemy of our soul tries to convince us are true, and they often outweigh the truth of what God has said.

People we encounter in life serve as the up-close-and-personal, imperfect conduits through which we receive the lies or the truth about how worthy we are to be loved and valued. Too often, we allow the love and acceptance we have failed to receive from others to become a distorted reflection of God's ability to love us.

Our parents serve as our first measuring stick of God's love. We enter this world entirely helpless, completely reliant upon those we belong to. Those to whom we have been entrusted are the most important people in our lives, the center of our world, and our first representation of God as Father. We need them, and we need them to meet our needs. Their love, care, and ultimate display of approval through meeting our needs are necessary for our survival.

Because we are created with this need to be loved, children often will conform to the demands of their parents, striving with all their might to obtain the love they so desperately desire. This struggle often continues into adulthood; little kids encased in adult bodies still driven by the innate desire to earn the love of their parents. This is an exhausting and unsatisfying journey as many parents, for various reasons, are incapable of giving the love their children need in the ways they need it.

From the moment we first open our eyes, we perceive our worth by what we receive from those who have the power to shape the way we think and feel, both about ourselves and about the world in which we live.

Having lacked words of affirmation in my childhood, I probably overdid this in the lives of my children. I was determined that they would always know they were loved. Without a shadow of a doubt, they would always feel secure, accepted, and cherished. From our first sacred moments together, I stared into their innocent little eyes and held them close, assuring them of the many things I wished someone had assured me of.

I love you.

I will love you always.

I will never leave you.

You are beautiful to me.

These are the very words our Heavenly Father speaks to us.

When our parents are able to love us well, we start with an established foundation of worth and value. These are the people who created us, and it stands to reason that if anyone on this earth "should" love us as God intended, it would be them. Unfortunately, this is not always the case. Often, parents are wounded children functioning in adult bodies. In the absence of receiving the healing and teaching that they needed to parent well, they lack the ability to give us what we need as their children. For a child who lives life with this type of parent, starting off on such shaky ground mentally and emotionally can put them on unstable ground with unsure footing for the remainder of their days.

And then there are the others; the broken, frail, and flawed human beings with whom we do life. We look for the love and approval of everyone from best friends to boyfriends, teachers to bosses, and pastors to mentors.

Humans being human, it doesn't take long at all for hurt, rejection, and abandonment to knock on the door of our heart. Because humans will always be imperfect reflections of the love of God, we will always have opportunities to be wounded in our walk with others.

Along the way, whether by choice or chance, as we trust and make ourselves vulnerable, we time and again give others the opportunity to indicate whether we are worth loving. Despite the specific circumstances of the life you have lived, people's actions have presented evidence countless times that you are not worth loving. Through judgment, criticism, condemnation, rejection, and abandonment in either word or deed, you have been given proof that who you are is not worth the love they have to give.

As a result, we take this "evidence" and transform it into the reality of our deservedness to be loved. It's easy to think that if these people who are supposed to love me don't do so, then I must not be worth loving. And yet, it's the opposite that's true. We simply must use the correct measuring stick.

Chapter Three

> *But God, who is rich in mercy, because of His great love with which He loved us, even when we were dead in trespasses, made us alive together with Christ.*
>
> **EPHESIANS 2:4–5**

We need to understand that people—whether they be our parents, our pastor, or our partner—are fallible, and their ability to love us will always be both tainted at worst and limited at best due to their own frail humanity. Understanding this, we can then begin to move in the direction of truth.

Here is the truth, beloved; all of the people in your life who have failed to love you have not done so on the basis of your unworthiness to be loved. Instead, their inability to love well is due to the unhealed, broken, and wounded places within them. It can be difficult to accept, but people do the very best they can.

Sometimes, that "best" seems to be the worst and, based on the needs, longings, and desires that God created within us, falls far short of what we believe their behavior should be. These things don't make you "needy," Daughter of God; they make you normal. We were created with a heart and soul that were intended by God to be cared for:

loved,

chosen,

forgiven,

seen,

led,

supplied.

We were created with a body that needs to be nourished. A deficit of nourishment results in malnourishment; malnourishment leads to abnormal growth patterns and, ultimately, a failure to thrive.

We were created with a soul that needs to be nourished. We were created to thrive, not just survive. When we do not receive the nourishment required for us to have a healthy soul, we live out of a place of malnourishment, always seeking that which we were created to have.

Let's use a basic example. There are places in this world where mamas don't have the ability to feed their children. A baby needs food to survive. However, no matter how much that mama loves her baby, no matter how much she would love nothing more than to be able to nourish it's frail, wasting-away body, she simply does not have the supply within her to meet the baby's needs.

That baby does what he knows to do to get his needs met. He looks to the one that is his source, and cries out. There is a lack of understanding within the heart of that baby as to why the very one he looks to refuses to give what he so desperately needs and desires. He can't comprehend why his source for all things and his supply have dried up.

By nature, children are egocentric; they are survivalists, utterly dependent on others to meet all their needs. Everything in their world is about them. Because they can't meet their own needs, they demand that others do so. When what was meant to be doesn't come to pass, they are at a loss of how to make sense of it.

Through no fault of their own, children are born self-centered, and the result of their needs not being met begins to form a belief within. This belief is that their own insufficiency in some area has caused this lack. They cry louder, kick harder, and flail bigger in order to get someone to know that they are in need. When they have done everything they know to do and it still doesn't suffice, it leaves them in a weary, confused place. It feels personal.

"Why is this happening?"

"What have I done wrong?"

"What am I doing wrong?"

"What do I need to do to get you to give me what I need, physically, emotionally, mentally, and spiritually?"

The cry of the infant becomes the acting out of the child—believing that if they could just be seen and heard, the provision would come.

The acting out of the child becomes the rebelliousness of the adolescent—a hardened heart that believes they have to meet their own needs.

The rebelliousness of the adolescent becomes the despondency of the adult—a loss of hope that their needs will be met.

And yet, the failure to provide the needs of the child isn't personal at all.

There's nothing the mama would want more.

There's nothing the baby would want more.

There's nothing that can be done.

Mama cannot give what she does not have.

Similarly, imperfect parents simply don't have within them what they need to nourish the hearts and souls of their children. We cannot give what we do not have.

Parents aren't the only ones who fail to meet our needs.

~ When the spouse cheats, failing to faithfully abide by the forever vow that they made.

~ When the child flees, failing to embrace the path that has been provided for them.

~ When the sibling disappoints, failing to fulfill the expectations of the role into which they were born.

~ When the friend falls short, failing to walk beside us well in the way we had hoped.

~ When the spiritual leader flails, falling off of the pedestal on which we have placed them.

In each place, the hurt we experience through the failures of others feels very personal, but it's not.

Adultery, rebellion, abandonment, and rejection are simply the result of those individuals searching to satisfy some unmet need within them.

When someone has hurt you, it's difficult to believe that they're doing their best, because what they've offered you is so very short of what should have been.

~ A mother should know how to love her baby.

~ A father should protect and provide.

~ A friend should be loyal and forgiving.

~ A Christian should reflect the character of Christ.

However, "should" is a word based on a world that runs the way it ought, and on lives filled with the wisdom and love of God poured out from one individual to another. What happens when the "shoulds" don't happen? The effects are painful and far-reaching. The ripples of unfulfilled longings for love cause humans to be unable, within themselves, to love others the way they "should."

Chapter Four

*This hope we have as an anchor of the soul,
a hope both sure and steadfast and one which
enters within the veil.*

HEBREWS 6:19 (NASB)

The women I encounter who have been abused or neglected by their parents frequently have parents who have been, in their own childhood, abused and neglected by someone. You see, we cannot give what we do not have.

You may wonder; is there any hope to be found in a dark and dying world filled with hurting and unhealed people? Is there any way to break the cycle of wounds that continue to be passed on from person to person?

Yes.

As in all things, our hope, our only hope, lies in the Lord of our Salvation. The rule of grim reality is broken by truly understanding and receiving His gracious love and, in turn, healing. Christ desires to use those who will allow Him to transform them, through His love and healing, from a place of brokenness to a place of wholeness. Through this transformation, we become a funnel of that very love and healing into the lives of others. His love, manifested in our hearts and lives, enables us to become vessels through which He pours His love into others as we yield to Him.

For those who have Christ as their Savior, there is a weaving of our ability with His in order to love others. When we so choose, He shines through us, helping us to give the love we have received from Him to those He brings across our path daily. And yet we have all failed, at one time or another, to love others well.

How does one move forward from this place of longing and striving for love? Where do we look when we do not receive the love we need from this earth?

Daughter of God, the more you embrace your identity as a daughter of the King, the more your feet will be firmly set and established on unshakable ground. This unshakable ground is the truth He shares time and again in His Word, the truth that you are worth loving because He has deemed it so. He sent His son to die for YOU. He did this knowing you fully, from the top of your head to the tips of your toes. He chose you first.

People are fickle. Their human love is based on so many different things. And yet, God's love is based solely on the fact that He IS love.

In 1 John 4:8, we see that "He who does not love does not know God, for God is love."

And 1 Corinthians 13:4–7 gives us a blueprint for exactly what that means.

You see, God knew that the demonstrations of love that we would experience on this earth through others would fall short of exhibiting the depth of His love for us. In His kindness, He very carefully laid out in understandable terms exactly what His kind of love looks like, what He looks like, and who He is. This is what God's love looks like:

> Love suffers long and is kind; love does not envy; love does not parade itself, is not puffed up; does not behave rudely, does not seek its own, is not provoked, thinks no evil; does not rejoice in iniquity, but rejoices in the truth; bears all things, believes all things, hopes all things, endures all things. (1 Corinthians 13: 4–7)

This is what love looks like and who God is. He IS love. Therefore, if anything we think about Him or His character contradicts the truth of His love, it cannot be true. In fact, any time we experience this kind of love through another human being, it is only because they are accessing God's love and sharing it with us. Anytime we are able to truly love, it is God's love poured out through us. Outside of that, we are incapable of demonstrating this kind of love.

So where do we go from here? We "know" in our brains that God loves us—we have read it and heard it and know what we are "supposed" to believe—but how do we get to standing firm upon that unshakable foundation? How do we live this life in the trust and confidence that God's Word is true in regard to His unfathomable, unshakable, never-changing love for us despite the way humans have loved us well or failed to do so?

The more we embrace our identity as a daughter of the King, the more people's inability to love us diminishes in importance in comparison to the love of God laid out for us in His Word. It has been clearly established. He IS love, and He loves US!

Chapter Five

> *He loved us first.*
> 1 JOHN 4:19 (MSG)

Many daughters of God struggle with believing that God could love them because they know themselves all too well. Their focus strays from magnifying the never-ending, never-changing love of God. Instead, they target the many places where they fall short of all that He has called them to be, from repetitive sin to hidden sin, and from long-lasting struggles to the inability to obey the elementary aspects of being a Christian. Being experts in falling short of the "shoulds"—and pros in the "shouldn'ts"—trips them up.

They are hindered in their ability to believe that in the very midst of all their imperfections, God could fully see, know, accept, and love them, right where they are on their journey with Jesus. They believe they should:

- ~ Read their Bible

- ~ Pray

- ~ Serve more

- ~ Not yell at their kids

- ~ Not be so impatient

- ~ Not be so judgmental

The list is endless, and our enemy is the best list maker. One of his favorite tactics is to keep us constantly self-focused; he works hard—using the laundry list of our inadequacies—to convince us that truly we aren't worthy of our title as "Daughter," and we really don't deserve the love of our Father.

But here is where our confidence as daughters of the King lies. He loved us FIRST. Before we loved Him. Before we even knew what the Christian hoops to jump through were. Before we did our first Bible study or prayer or fast. He LOVED us. His love never was and never will be based on lists of things that we do right or wrong. His love has only ever been based on the unchanging truth that He IS love. He can never and will never be anything but love.

In Jeremiah 1:5, the Lord tells us that He knew us in our mother's womb.

He knew us.

You are no surprise to Him, dear one. When He designed you and chose to call you His own, He knew exactly what He was getting. He knew your strengths and weaknesses. He knew your personality. He knew all of the places you would struggle, and He knew all of the places you would have victory. He knew the beautifully unique ways that you would bring Him glory, and He knew every opportunity that you would miss. He loved you still. He loves you because He deemed you worthy to be loved.

When we refuse to embrace the truth that He unconditionally and unequivocally loves us, we elevate our own opinion, or the opinion of others, above God's opinion. Believing that we are seen, known, and loved is the foundational cornerstone to embracing our identity as a daughter of the King. Everything He has done for us is because He loves us. Our whole relationship with Him is based on how very much He loves us. Until we can understand and accept this foundational truth and what it means, we are unable to effectively move forward into the other important aspects of our identity in Him.

If we struggle to believe that He loves us, then how can we believe that He chooses to use us?

Or forgive us?

Or heal us?

GOD IS UNCHANGING.

Jesus Christ is the same yesterday, today, and forever. (Hebrews13:8)

GOD'S LOVE FOR US IS UNCHANGING.

Yet in all these things we are more than conquerors through Him who loved us. For I am persuaded that neither death nor life, nor angels nor principalities nor powers, nor things present nor things to come, nor height nor depth, nor any other created thing, shall be able to separate us from the love of God which is in Christ Jesus our Lord. (Romans 8:37–39)

People are imperfect. Their ability to walk in love often is determined by a variation of life and circumstances and the difficulties and struggles they are facing. A great demonstration of this is found in parenting. One day, our children can behave a certain way and we respond with love, kindness, and patience, just as the parenting books have told us to do. The very next day, because we are tired, overwhelmed, or busy, that very same behavior can elicit a response that would better demonstrate how not to parent. We are all susceptible to the fluctuations that arise from the storms of this life. God, however, is not.

He is ALWAYS the same.

Never changing.

Never wavering.

Never is His response to us determined by any factor outside of Him being love, and loving us.

We can firmly plant our feet in that assurance and face with confidence whatever is before us.

His love is always available for us to run to, rely on, and rest in.

Chapter Six

Let all that you do be done in love.
1 CORINTHIANS 16:14 (NASB)

I didn't love my husband when we got married. It sounds horrible to say, but it's true. After a year of dating, including three months of engagement, we stood at the altar, said sacred vows before both God and man, and committed our till-death-do-we-part love to one another.

Looking back, I realize that even though I thought I loved him, I was really in love with the idea of being loved by him. I was desperate to be above all others in his heart and life for the remainder of mine. I was nineteen; my frame of reference regarding love was limited at best and distorted at worst.

Twenty-two years later, I believe that I have now at least begun to understand the deep intertwining of what love is. I found and pieced various aspects of it together along the way to offer a clearer yet still incomplete picture. As we live out the rest of our lives together, I pray that perhaps one day I will know the fullness of what it means to truly love another human being with all that they are, to the very depths of their soul, for their whole life.

Although I know now that it has taken place, I am unable to pinpoint a specific time for that transition from not really loving to loving. I do know where it didn't happen, though. It wasn't the result of beautiful flowers sent, decadent chocolates presented, or even memorable, romantic weekend getaways. It also wasn't found in quaint candlelight dinners or soft satin sheets amidst the throes of passion.

Instead, I believe it was gleaned from and accumulated in many different kinds of moments. Moments of commitment through heartache, communication so difficult it demanded tears, and forgiveness that lacked an "I told you so." This is where I found love.

My relationship with my husband serves as an adequate metaphor for my relationship with my Lord. In my teens, I confessed with my mouth and believed in my heart that Jesus was my Lord... but I didn't really love Him. I was thankful for the security of eternal salvation, daily-renewed grace, and a robe of righteousness to replace my rags of filth, but the truth is, I was primarily focused on Him loving and saving me and thought very little about the reciprocal. A selfish, self-serving love isn't really love at all.

I cannot pinpoint the exact moment of transition, but I know that it has occurred. It wasn't found in the moments of abundant blessings, exuberant celebrations of His goodness, or mountaintop experiences of favor poured out. My heart remains so thankful, and yet, those are not the places where my love for Him became real.

Instead, it has accumulated in many different kinds of moments. Moments of undeserved grace. Moments of commitment through heartache, communication so difficult it demanded tears, and forgiveness that lacked an "I told you so."

My love for both my God and my husband became most real within me when my heart's focus shifted from what they could do for me to what I could do for them. True love requires an unwavering commitment, sacrifice, and willingness to serve wholeheartedly.

True love is demanding, requiring that the giver hold nothing back.

True love never disappoints because it is in the giving that you receive.

While reading John 4, I can't help but think that LOVE—real love, true love—is not always rainbows and sunshine. Sometimes love is hard truth given as gently as possible. Sometimes love is the willingness to bear the brunt of another's hurt and clean up the mess you didn't make. Sometimes love is well-set boundaries, and sometimes it's looking another in the eye and laying it all out for them right at the bottom line. Sometimes love is refusing to allow someone to treat you in a way that is not acceptable because they need to learn that it's not okay, and no one else has ever loved them enough to stand up to them.

And then there are the things that love always does: (Lines in bold taken from 1 Corinthians 13:4–8 MSG.)

LOVE NEVER GIVES UP.

~ Not even on people that make your eyeballs itch.

LOVE CARES MORE FOR OTHERS THAN FOR SELF.

~ Even when they care more about themselves than about you.

LOVE DOESN'T WANT WHAT IT DOESN'T HAVE.

~ Even when it seems completely unfair and illogical that someone else would have it.

LOVE DOESN'T STRUT.

~ Because we know that anything we have of value is only due to God's grace and favor.

DOESN'T HAVE A SWELLED HEAD.

~ Because it's not about us but about Him in us.

DOESN'T FORCE ITSELF ON OTHERS.

~ Because God is a gentleman, and we should strive to be like Him.

ISN'T ALWAYS "ME FIRST."

~ Because we are to think of others before ourselves.

DOESN'T FLY OFF THE HANDLE.

~ Because we are to treat others the way we would like to be treated.

DOESN'T KEEP SCORE OF THE SINS OF OTHERS.

~ Because in the same measure that we have received forgiveness, we should give.

DOESN'T REVEL WHEN OTHERS GROVEL.

~ Because we should hold the heart of God toward them.

TAKES PLEASURE IN THE FLOWERING OF TRUTH.

~ Even when it's hard, life-changing, and unrelenting.

PUTS UP WITH ANYTHING.

~ Because God puts up with us.

TRUSTS GOD ALWAYS.

~ Even when we don't understand, because no one is more trustworthy.

ALWAYS LOOKS FOR THE BEST.

~ Because God valued each of us enough to die for us.

NEVER LOOKS BACK.

~ Because that never helps you get where you want to go.

KEEPS GOING TO THE END.

~ No matter how much time or energy it takes.

It seems to me that, in the body of Christ, we have often come to confuse real love for false, in-your-face kindness. The truth, however, is that real love can be hard, unpleasant, and uncomfortable.

For most of us, our own lives can be consuming, distracting, and so very FULL that to take the time, energy, and perseverance necessary to really love our brothers and sisters in Christ often requires more than we have or want to give. Yet in John 13:35, we are told that the world is supposed to be able to recognize that we are disciples of Christ by our love for one another.

The absence of love leaves room for offenses, unforgiveness, and strife to rear their ugly heads and take control of situations, circumstances, and relationships. John reminds us:

> And we have known and believed the love that
> God has for us. God is love, and he who abides in
> love abides in God, and God in him. (1 John 4:16)

You simply cannot give away what you do not have, Daughter of God. It's not your fault; it's just impossible. Instead of realizing and accepting this truth, many daughters of the King repeat that endless cycle of identifying where they fall short of loving others, beating themselves up for it, trying hard to fix it, and then failing again.

It's time for a new cycle. When you embrace the truth of how very much God loves you fully and completely, just as you are right this second, His love will more freely flow through you into the lives of others.

You do not serve a God who is interested only in how He can impact others through you. He longs for you to know how deeply He loves you because He knows that truth is THE cornerstone of the foundation necessary for you to have or even desire the intimate relationship He desires to have with you. It is the pivotal first step of embracing the fullness of all the good things He has prepared for you, which He so desperately desires you to receive. Because He loves you, He longs—even more than you do—for you to walk in the peace, joy, and purpose for which He created you.

He's never too busy or too distracted to spend time with you. He cares about every single innate facet of your life. You are the object of His never-ending, never-faltering affection. He thinks you're great! You are His favorite you. He wants your heart—all of it, good, bad, and ugly. That won't change even if you never change. Because He loves you, He will never take from you what you are not willing to give.

Daughter of God, begin to embrace the love He has for you today.

PRAYER

Father, thank You for Your love—love that I could never earn and don't deserve. Thank you that You love me right where I am, just as I am—good, bad, and ugly. You always have and always will. No matter what happens in my life, I know that this is something that will not change and cannot change because You never change. Help me, Father, to receive Your love today and everyday.

YOU ARE LOVED
Questions for Journal & Discussion

1. Have you ever had, or do you now have, a hard time accepting and truly believing in God's unconditional love for you?

2. Do you believe that something you have done or continue to do disqualifies you from His love or makes it difficult for Him to love you?

3. How does your walk with Christ demonstrate to others what you believe about His love?

4. Who in your life has been a positive or negative conduit of God's love? In what way?

5. Is there a place in your life that you have held back from the Father due to fear of Him not being able to love you there? If so, are you willing to lay it before Him and allow Him access to bring healing, peace, and joy with the power of His unconditional love?

SECTION TWO
You Are Forgiven

For He made Him who knew no sin to be sin for us, that we might become the righteousness of God in Him.

2 CORINTHIANS 5:21

Chapter Seven

> *And if by grace, then it is no longer of works;*
> *otherwise grace is no longer grace. But if it is of works,*
> *it is no longer grace; otherwise work is no longer work.*
>
> **ROMANS 11:6**

It's interesting, this mindset the daughters of God seem to carry in relation to His grace, mercy, and forgiveness within their lives. Those with a heart for the lost would be quick to assure a non-believer, or a believer who is struggling, of His immeasurable grace and mercy upon their lives. Any evangelistic encourager would be eager to share the "come as you are" message to someone who believed that they had to be "all cleaned up" or have their act together before getting saved. Most would vehemently assure someone straddling the fence between born again and unsaved that there was nothing they had done or could ever do that would negate God's unconditional love and acceptance of them. It's the assurance that God loves and forgives them the good, the bad, and the ugly, and that they could, with one choice, live free to be...

completely seen,

completely known,

completely forgiven,

completely loved.

And yet, those same daughters of God seem to forget that the very same grace that is extended to an unbeliever remains strong and intact after someone has embraced the gift of adoption by their Heavenly Father. All too often, after choosing to believe that Jesus died for their sins, they also begin to believe that accepting their position as princess somehow negates the very same grace that ripped off their filthy rags and replaced them with a robe of righteousness in the first place. All too quickly there is an exchange. The "come as you are" message is traded in for the "you better get it right" message. Hope in Christ and what He has done has been replaced with the fear of messing up and falling out of His good graces.

How can it be that the simplicity of the gospel of accepting Jesus into your heart is enough to usher you into the kingdom of God... and yet not be enough to keep you there? Why are we so very eager to manufacture hoops to jump through to stay in His good graces?

As you therefore have received Christ Jesus the Lord, so walk in Him, rooted and built up in Him and established in the faith, as you have been taught, abounding in it with thanksgiving. (Colossians 2:6–7)

When I taught elementary school, I enjoyed having a classroom theme. For years, it was bees. I referred to my students as busy bees and encouraged them to *bee* kind to one another.

After two years of bee references and bee-ing surrounded by yellow and black, I decided that it was time for a change. Exchanging beehives for lily pads, I encouraged my students to embrace all things F-R-O-G. Besides reminding them to "Fully Rely On God," I was also able to sprinkle, throughout the day, encouragements to "hop to it," as well as praising them for "toad-a-ly awesome" behavior.

As a teacher, it's common to have a classroom behavior chart. In my classroom, our behavior management chart coincided with our classroom theme. Each of my students had their own little frog with their name written on it. Every morning, their frog would begin on the "first" lily pad on the back of our classroom door, and each major infraction of the rules resulted in them having to "hop their frog" to subsequent lily pads, each representing its own set of growing consequences.

Once a frog had been hopped, there was no redemption. Each student also carried home a sheet sporting a daily frog sticker if they had not ventured off the first lily pad. This helped me to easily communicate with parents the type of behavior their child had had that day. Eight frog stickers earned a trip to Mrs. Glanzman's treasure chest. Frog stickers were a daily topic of conversation and a *really big deal*.

The unfortunate hopping of a frog was known to catapult a child into tears or a tantrum. A trip to the treasure chest never elicited anything less than a whoop and jumping up and down in excitement. Each day, the big question from parents in the car loop was: "Did you get your frog?"

The frog chart was completely works based. It was when the children did everything that they were supposed to, and little that they were not, that they earned the frog their hearts coveted.

WE ALL HAVE FROGS IN OUR LIFE.

Our frogs at work come through kudos and paychecks, with an occasional promotion. Our frogs within relationships come when we treat others the way we should and meet the expectations that they have for us. Even the body of Christ has frogs. They come when you serve humbly and faithfully, all while jumping through the man-made hoops held by those who award themselves the right to judge and condemn. Frogs are everywhere, and they have become such an ingrained part of our thinking and way of living that we don't even recognize them anymore. What is life without frogs?

So foreign is it to consider a life not embodied by works that when we come to Christ, our whole way of thinking must be revamped. Almost from birth, we are trained and molded to "be good" and "do good" so that we can partake in whatever earthly benefits exist.

In contrast, God's kingdom is frog-free. When we accept Jesus Christ into our heart as our Lord and Savior, we are gifted with righteousness; this is like an eternally earned frog sticker.

> *The debt is paid,*
>
> *the mark is met,*
>
> *the work is done.*

No longer are we forced into striving to earn acceptance, love, or forgiveness. The treasure to be had is far more magnificent than anything found in a treasure chest. Instead, it provides unhindered access to the never-ending love of—and a relationship with—an unfailing, never-changing, merciful Father.

The price Christ paid by dying on the cross was completely sufficient to deal with the eternal consequence of every sin you will ever commit. It includes those you committed before accepting Christ as your Savior as well as those committed after.

For He made Him who knew no sin to be sin for us, that we might become the righteousness of God in Him. (2 Corinthians 5:21)

The sacrifice of Christ's life upon the cross has freed us to live life without frogs.

Surely He has borne our griefs
And carried our sorrows;
Yet we esteemed Him stricken,
Smitten by God, and afflicted.
But He was wounded for our transgressions,
He was bruised for our iniquities;
The chastisement for our peace was upon Him,
And by His stripes we are healed.
All we like sheep have gone astray;
We have turned, every one, to his own way;
And the Lord has laid on Him the iniquity of us all. (Isaiah 53:4–6)

Through accepting Him as our Savior and the acceptable sacrifice for all of our sin, we have been given access to the abundant treasures of the Kingdom of God.

The kingdom of God is not eating and drinking, but righteousness and peace and joy in the Holy Spirit. (Romans 14:17)

A life filled with righteousness, peace, and joy is the heart's desire of every daughter of the King.

Chapter Eight

*Being justified freely by His grace through the
redemption that is in Christ Jesus.*

ROMANS 3:24

My husband does the bills.

It was decided that he would do so during the
initial attempt at conjoining our bank accounts prior
to marriage, and we were excited at such a significant
representation of unity. Our premarital giddiness waned,
however, as the dignified teller kindly but firmly shared
that my personal account was overdrawn to the tune
of $270.00 and could not be closed until it was in the
black. Waiting patiently while I pulled out my checkbook
registry, it didn't matter to her that, according to my
figures, I had well over one hundred dollars to contribute
to our new joint account.

Graciously, my husband-to-be discreetly dealt with the issue. He paid the debt I owed and never spoke of it again. It was clear, however, with my apparent weakness in checkbook balancing, that he should oversee the family finances.

Since then, I have gotten into the practice of not even looking at the bills. When they come in the mail, I simply place them on my husband's desk to deal with as he sees fit. After twenty-three years of marriage, it has become the routine.

We're now past the years when finances were so tight that paying the bills called for nausea, tension, and mutual encouragement that God would see us through, and bill-paying has become routine.

At least I thought so until one day, from his bill-paying spot, my husband sweetly called my name. When I walked into the room, he held up a single bill, upon which I recognized the logo of our cell service provider. Even without him saying a word, I recognized those defining features of frustration etched across his face. I sat down on the bed, prepared to hear his venting about the cell phone company, the mistake they had made, and how he was going to have to deal with it.

After a moment of silence and a long, deliberate breath, he stated in a steady, calm voice, "Our cell phone bill shows that your telephone number went over our limit by 250 minutes." While I sat there, frozen in that deer-in-the-headlights stance, the awareness of talking on the phone a tad more than usual in the past month immediately started to resonate within me.

Realizing the dire financial consequences of such carelessness, I cautiously met his eyes, prepared to offer an acknowledgment of and an apology for my complete irresponsibility. He had every right to be frustrated with me. Aware that I was about to speak, he held up his hand to stop me. I braced myself, preparing for the remainder of whatever he had to offer.

With kind eyes and a soft but serious tone, he said, "Let's try to be more careful about that... okay?" I replied, "Okay." What else could I say? He then turned back to the computer screen, indicating our conversation was finished and I was "off the hook."

I spent the rest of the day contemplating my husband's response of goodness and grace. He could have reacted so much differently. I was well aware of the magnitude of the mistake made. Had he responded any other way, I might have become defensive or made excuses. Yet, his kind response to me did not cause me to dismiss the seriousness of my mistake. The goodness and grace of his response served only to magnify my desire to never make that mistake again.

FORGIVEN MUCH

God's grace has that same effect on me.

The story we find in Luke 7:36–50 is one of my favorites.

Then one of the Pharisees asked Him to eat with him. And He went to the Pharisee's house, and sat down to eat.

And behold, a woman in the city who was a sinner, when she knew that Jesus sat at the table in the Pharisee's house, brought an alabaster flask of fragrant oil, and stood at His feet behind Him weeping; and she began to wash His feet with her tears, and wiped them with the hair of her head; and she kissed His feet and anointed them with the fragrant oil.

Now when the Pharisee who had invited Him saw this, he spoke to himself saying, "This Man, if He were a prophet, would know who and what manner of woman this is who is touching Him, for she is a sinner."

And Jesus answered and said to him, "Simon, I have something to say to you." So he said, "Teacher, say it."

"There was a certain creditor who had two debtors. One owed five hundred denarii, and the other fifty. And when they had nothing with which to repay, he freely forgave them both. Tell Me, therefore, which of them will love him more?"

Simon answered and said, "I suppose the one whom he forgave more."

And He said to him, "You have rightly judged."

Then He turned to the woman and said to Simon, "Do you see this woman? I entered your house; you gave Me no water for My feet, but she has washed My feet with her tears and wiped them with the hair of her head. You gave Me no kiss, but this woman has not ceased to kiss My feet since the time I came in. You did not anoint My head with oil, but this woman has anointed My feet with fragrant oil. Therefore I say to you, her sins, which are many, are forgiven, for she loved much. But to whom little is forgiven, the same loves little."

Then He said to her, "Your sins are forgiven."

And those who sat at the table with Him began to say to themselves, "Who is this who even forgives sins?"

Then He said to the woman, "Your faith has saved you. Go in peace."

I love this story because I am so easily able to identify with that woman.

Having had a dysfunctional family and a childhood filled with neglect and tremendous abuse, there was much to be forgiven by the time I chose to serve the Lord as a young adult. Where some might struggle to see their need for a Savior due to their life appearing to be that of a "good" person, the depth of my need for grace and mercy was as apparent to me as a bright blinking sign that screamed, SINNER!

Because I have been forgiven much, I love much.

All have sinned and have fallen short of the glory of God and therefore need a Savior. (Romans 3:23 AP)

Not all that come to the cross, however, have had the same life experiences or circumstances. The various things we have been through helped shape us into the person we have become. In my own life, the pain and instability of childhood contributed to many of the choices I made. The knowledge of these poor choices made it difficult for me to embrace my identity as a daughter of the King. Promiscuity, an eating disorder, and self-harm are only some of the issues I brought to the cross to lay at the feet of Jesus.

It is a misconception that, once you accept Jesus as Lord and Savior, you are immediately unburdened from the emotional baggage you possess. You carry it all with you into the Kingdom, that which has been handed to you by others or that you have picked up along the journey of life.

Once we begin our journey with Jesus, the truth in 2 Corinthians 5:17 tells us that we become a new creation;

we are empowered to overcome anything in our life that isn't beneficial or life-giving. Some things we overcome more quickly than others.

What we can know beyond a shadow of a doubt is that with Christ in us, nothing is impossible for us as we continue yielding our hearts and lives to Him. We can be confident that He will be faithful to continue the good work that He has begun within us.

> Being confident of this, that he who began a good work in you will carry it on to completion until the day of Christ Jesus. (Philippians 1:6 NIV)

Chapter Nine

> *He will be faithful to continue the good work*
> *that He has begun within us.*
>
> **PHILIPPIANS 1:6 (AP)**

Because we continue to struggle with certain issues, faults, and sins even after we accept Christ, we can allow the enemy of our soul to convince us that we are not really daughters of the King who are worthy to be loved by Him. Although He tells us in Hebrews 4:16 to come boldly to His throne of grace so "that we may obtain mercy and find grace to help in time of need," we can be deceived into thinking that if we struggle in the same place too long, our invitation to the throne gets revoked.

By attacking our identity as a Beloved Daughter of God, the enemy encourages us to "kink our own hose," finding ourselves, again and again, trying to self-help rather than sprinting full-force to the only one who can really help us live the way He has called us to live. Until we realize that there is no better place for us than at His feet in the very midst of our repetitive sin and struggles, we will continue to struggle. If we had the ability to make ourselves "all better," we wouldn't have needed a Savior to begin with.

Knowing it was important to get up early but realizing that my body wasn't cooperating, I got into the shower to help things along. As the water started, so did my brain, shifting straight into third gear. Scrolling through the tasks of the day ahead, I began the motions of daily cleansing. Barely cognitive of purposeful action, the individual tasks involved were less intentional and more instinctual: wash my body, wash my face, wash my hair. Although the color, smell, and texture of cleansing goop changed, the routine never did.

As soon as I placed shampoo onto my head and began to lather, I was distracted from my inner dialogue by the distinctive sense of déjà vu. With only a few finger scrunches, the quick intensity of lather confirmed that I had already washed my hair. I was irritated that now I would have to take time to go through the entire process yet again.

It's not that washing my hair is difficult; my frustration was aimed at the pointless redundancy of repeating an act I had already completed. The time, energy, and shampoo wasted because of my absentmindedness and lack of attention scrubbed me the wrong way.

This isn't the only area of my life that has been touched by needless repetition.

For years, I was stuck in the wash, rinse, and repeat cycle. When I would sin, the gentle, loving conviction of God would be smothered by the gut-wrenching condemnation offered to me by the enemy of my soul.

Like a shamed and fearful child, sometimes days and even weeks would go by that I would avoid time alone with my Heavenly Father. It was a self-imposed exile in expectation of His disappointment, frustration, and irritation that once again I had failed, fallen short, and missed the mark.

Eyes and heart cast down, I would listen and accept each scornful accusation from the enemy reassuring me that I had surely blown it this time. Although I could feel the Holy Spirit tugging at me to come and spend time with Him, I would decline His gentle invitation, reminding Him of how unworthy I was of His love, forgiveness, and mercy. I embraced the self-inflicted pain of isolation from my Father. I believed I deserved to suffer.

Often, in the aftermath of failure, children experience rejection from the authority figures in their life, and a belief system forms that makes rejection in the face of failure the most comfortable to them.

Eventually, I would find myself again at the realization that God was both my breath and my life.

Where did I have to go but to Him? Always with abundant tears and a contrite heart, I would slowly make my way to His throne room of grace and gently knock on the door, entering with head down and eyes averted. I couldn't understand why He would want to spend time with me, as we both knew exactly who I was. He patiently listened to my guilt-ridden confessions—choked out between sobs of anger and frustration—of where I found myself yet again due to my willful disobedience.

Out of words and exhausted from the intensity of the moment, I would then just lie there, swimming in the truth of how unworthy I was of any kindness, mercy, or love that He would extend to me.

Then peace would come, and

He would speak to my heart.

He would remind me of His love for me. That He was both my Alpha and Omega, knowing my beginning and my end. Even so, He loved me first, with my every flaw and imperfection, and that was the reason I loved Him. He assured me that my choices were no surprise to Him. He knew what He was getting when He chose me, called me, and set me apart as His own.

"I love you, and you are forgiven:

go and sin no more."

Chapter Ten

> *O Lord, you have searched me and known me.*
> **PSALM 139:1**

You see, Daughter of the King, He knew exactly what He was getting when He got you. Your struggles are no surprise to Him, and He fails to fall off the throne when you fail to walk in the fullness of the life to which He has called you.

In fact, right in the very midst of your sin, whether hidden or seen by others, He loves you, and His mercy and grace are sufficient.

> Through the Lord's mercies we are not consumed, because His compassions fail not. They are new every morning; Great is Your faithfulness. (Lamentations 3:22–23)

For some, it is hard to believe that, despite our weaknesses, He loves us still. We can feel that one who calls herself a Daughter of the King should have her act together and should not struggle with the same things repeatedly. Expressing outwardly that we know it's true, inwardly we struggle with accepting His unconditional love, mercy, and grace.

We believe God loves us even though He knows about us what we know about ourselves: the good, the bad, and the ugly. The enemy, however, is always happy to help convince us that we are beyond God's ability to fully love us.

Even though we desire in our hearts to be perfect and to honor Him with all of our days and all of our ways, time and time again we fall short. We can begin to believe that God is angry, frustrated, or disappointed with us for not being who we should be. Guilt and condemnation move in, causing us to turn our face and our eyes away from Him.

However, as seen in Romans 2:4, it is the goodness of God that draws us to repentance.

In the very midst of our yuck, He longs for us to crawl up in His lap, lay our head against His chest, and be loved by Him. The more we see ourselves as He sees us—fully loved, fully accepted, and fully forgiven, right where we are on our journey with Him—the more we are transformed into the daughter of God He has called us to be.

The worst types of illnesses for little ones seem to be tummy related. Those unpleasant issues, mixed with a snuffy nose, make for long days and even longer nights for the parents of a sick child. Unable to tend to their own needs, it seems that at these times they just leak all over, occasionally erupting from one place or another.

I remember feeling helpless in those early years, with my first child burning with fever and crying nonstop. All efforts to soothe her misery seemed futile. Cycling through the motions of rocking to swaying to walking, hour upon hour, we would find only pockets of sleep to ease our weariness.

My sweet husband, seeing how miserable she was and how exhausted we both were, stood by helplessly, wishing there was something he could do to help either one of us. We previously had learned, however, that when the baby was sick, she wanted her mama. No one else would do.

Occasionally, we would find merciful respite when the medicine kicked in and eased her symptoms. Knowing that to lay her in her crib would be self-defeating, I gently positioned her on my chest and settled my head back against the recliner. In what seemed like only moments, we would both be awakened by coughing, gagging, and vomiting.

I would have to quickly hand her to her father to clean up. When out of my arms, her crying immediately escalated from a steady, "I am so miserable; why is this happening to me?" cry to an all-out, raging scream.

Every second I could see her reaching her arms out to me and calling my name, "Mama, Mama!" through her tears was a painful eternity to my heart. I longed to hold her and bring her the comfort she needed.

In those times, I never even considered how my daughter's illness would impact me. Would I catch what she had? Would I be puked on, snotted on, or, potentially, even worse? Probably. It didn't matter. All I could think about when she was holding her arms out for me was how very much I loved her and how I longed to give her the comfort she desired. My heart hurt because she hurt.

As a child of God, there have been seasons when, very much like my sick little girl, my own heart symptoms have been unlovely. I was happy to run to God when I felt strong and obedient, but in my moments of weakness, disobedience, and un-loveliness (those times when, in truth, I needed God the most), I would withdraw my heart from Him because I did not feel worthy of His love and forgiveness.

I had to learn that I am not a better parent than my Lord. When we are weak and needy, our Father longs to be the comfort that we need. He knows our faults and weaknesses, but no matter how unlovely we seem, He always sees us with the heart of a loving parent. When we hurt, He hurts for us, even when it's through our own poor or disobedient choices that we are experiencing hurt. Mercy and compassion abound toward His children, especially in our times of weakness. As Romans 6:23 tells us:

> For the wages of sin is death, but the gift of God
> is eternal life in Christ Jesus our Lord.

Chapter Eleven

> *For sin shall not have dominion over you,*
> *for you are not under law but under grace.*
> ROMANS 6:14

The goal, beautiful Daughter of the King, is that we would not sin. The reason our loving Heavenly Father has laid out boundaries for us in His Word is twofold. First, His purpose is to help us recognize our need for a Savior. Secondly, He loves us so very much that His heart's desire would be for us always to make choices that lead to life and truth within our lives. Because He loves us so very much, He has done His best to lay out His plan for us to experience the absolute best life possible.

All sin has consequences. When we fall short of living the life He desires for us by making poor choices and being disobedient, we suffer the consequences of those choices. Many times in my office, I see people who are in the midst of suffering the consequences of choices they have made. In the pain of what they are going through, they struggle to run to God for help because they believe that the consequences they are experiencing are the direct result of God punishing them.

God tells us ahead of time that if we choose to be disobedient to the truths He has laid out for us, we will suffer consequences. Each time we sin, we inadvertently open the door to the enemy to bring destruction and torment into our lives.

And yet, God is faithful still.

I offer this analogy to my clients: When my children were little, I taught them not to run into the street. My motive was not to hinder their freedom for the sake of imposing rules, but instead, to keep them safe. I knew things about the road that they did not. I knew the dangers of oncoming traffic and how quickly out-of-sight vehicles could emerge. I loved them, and because of that, I wanted to keep them safe, even from danger they could not see.

And yet, if one of my children had run out into the street and gotten struck by a car, a herd of elephants could not have held me back from sprinting to them, scooping them up, and doing whatever I needed to do to help them. Despite my many warnings and their disobedience to my teaching, I would not stand on the side of the road and let them know that they got what they deserved. I would not ask three more cars to run over them to make sure they learned their lesson.

I wouldn't have been the one that issued the consequences to their disobedience. Getting hit by a car is a natural consequence of running out into the road. As a good Mama, I would hurt for their hurt while they experienced the pain of their disobedience, all the while holding them close and assuring them that I loved them, and I was going to stay by their side until they healed. Any good parent would respond in kind.

Our Heavenly Father is a good Father. A better parent than I could ever be. In Psalm 103:13–14, He reminds us that He is compassionate and remembers that we are but dust, and in Hebrews 4:15, He tells us that He sympathizes with our weaknesses.

> I will greatly rejoice in the Lord,
> My soul shall be joyful in my God;
> For He has clothed me with the
> garments of salvation,
> He has covered me with the robe of righteousness,
> As a bridegroom decks himself with ornaments,
> And as a bride adorns herself with her jewels.
> (Isaiah 61:10)

When my children were attending school, they were required to wear school uniforms; nothing fancy, just your typical khakis and navy-blue polo. There were many times that I was thankful for this requirement simply because it made my life easier. There were never any early morning, sleepy-eyed battles regarding what they would wear for school, and shopping for school clothes could not have been less complicated.

We decided that, at age eight, it was time for our son to become more independent in his clothing choices. He was required to practice choosing appropriate clothing both for play and for church.

Playtime apparel wasn't an issue because any pair of shorts and a tee-shirt worked for me. I didn't even care if they matched and was just happy to see him develop his ability to make reasonable choices. Church, however, was a bit different. The first Sunday he came downstairs after dressing himself, I was prepared to gently and lovingly send him back upstairs to "try again," if needed.

It took me a moment to process when he walked into the kitchen with a broad grin on his face, happily adorned in his school uniform: khaki pants, navy polo. Because we attended a church where formal dress was not required, Tyler's school uniform was quite appropriate attire. He was pleased with himself at "getting it right the first time," and I was pleased that he was pleased with his independent decision-making skills.

The following Sunday, Tyler again had the opportunity to choose his own church clothes... and again, he came downstairs in his school uniform. This was one of those "mommy moments" when I really had to evaluate what was important and what the motives of my heart were.

The fact was that Tyler was continuing to choose something appropriate for church, in an independent manner. These were the guidelines that had been laid out before him. The issue now became more about whether or not I felt comfortable in giving him the freedom to choose, even if it meant that he chose to wear his school uniform to church every Sunday for the rest of his life.

Our Heavenly Father has generously and graciously dressed us as His children. A beautiful robe of righteousness awaits each child of God who chooses to humbly and willingly submit their hearts and lives, accepting the new identity that is theirs according to the inheritance they have received.

Often, however, we are tempted by the enemy of our souls to toss aside our robe of righteousness and replace it with something much less fitting. He tries to whisper in our ear that a robe of shame, insufficiency, or self-defeat really suits us better. He even helps us put it on, step by step, attempting to convince us the entire time that this is what we were intended to wear all along. His desire is for us to believe that we were never worthy of a robe of righteousness to begin with.

What robe are you wearing today,

dear Daughter of the Most High King?

Are you dressed appropriately according to the royalty you are... or are you trying to wear spiritual and emotional clothes that were never intended for you?

Daily, as we remind ourselves of who we are in Christ, we must choose to surround ourselves with the robe of righteousness that our Father has so lovingly chosen for us as a gift of grace. Regarding our choice of spiritual clothing, our Father would always prefer for us to remain dependent upon Him to dress us in His righteousness rather than choosing something much less fitting.

And yet, God loves us so much that He never forces us to choose what He would choose for us. In Him, there is freedom and liberty. He is love, and there is no room for bondage or control in love. We are, of course, always better off when we make choices led by His wisdom.

I know I've made choices many times that we both knew were not the best. There have even been times when I knew the Holy Spirit was leading me in a different direction, and because of pride, fear, or just plain old stubbornness, I chose my own way instead.

I also know that whatever choices I've made, wherever they've led me, He has never left my side. He continues to love and encourage me, even when I choose differently than He would choose for me.

As we continue to do our best to live the life He has called us to live, running to Him in our moments of weakness, allowing Him access to every part of who we are, He will continue the good work He has begun in us. The longer we continue to journey with Jesus, wrapping our Father-issued robes of righteousness tightly around our shoulders and intentionally embracing our identity as a daughter of the King, the more we will look like, act like, and feel like who we truly are:

Our Father's Daughter.

Daughter of God, your Father knows you. He loves you. He accepts you. Right where you are on your journey with Him. When He looks at you, He sees you as "holy, and blameless, and above reproach" (Colossians 1:22).

The more time you spend with Him, learning about who He is and allowing His love and truth to transform you into His image, the more you will begin to see yourself as He sees you: A fully seen, fully known, and fully loved daughter of God.

Daughter of God, embrace His forgiveness today.

PRAYER

Father, thank you for Your forgiveness—grace and mercy like I've never known before. Thank you that because of what Jesus has done for me on the cross, I am now pure, holy, and blameless in Your sight. Thank you, Father, that You strengthen me in my weak places to obey Your Word so that I am able to live the life of freedom, joy, and peace You have created me to live.

YOU ARE FORGIVEN
Questions for Journal & Discussion

1. Are you able to recognize any FROGS in your life? If so, where do you feel the need to work harder to earn acceptance and affirmation? Do you struggle with the fear of failure?

2. Is there a place where you have struggled to accept the forgiveness of your Father? Are you willing to accept the forgiveness He has for you today?

3. When you are faced with your own struggles and failures, do you have a habit of running to God, or away from God? Are there ways that you could more fully or quickly embrace the truth of unconditional love and forgiveness in those moments?

4. Who has been the best example of God's forgiveness in your life? Are there places where God's forgiveness can flow more freely through you into the lives of others?

5. What does your "wardrobe" look like on a daily basis? Is it robes of shame and condemnation chosen by the enemy of your soul, or robes of royalty and righteousness chosen for you by your Father King?

SECTION THREE
You Are Chosen

*You did not choose Me, but I chose you
and appointed you that you should
go and bear fruit, and that your fruit
should remain, so that whatever you ask
the Father in My name He may give you.*

JOHN 15:16

Chapter Twelve

> *But you are a chosen generation, a royal priesthood,*
> *a holy nation, His own special people, that you may*
> *proclaim the praises of Him who called you out of*
> *darkness into His marvelous light.*
>
> 1 PETER 2:9

Chosen!

It's what we have all longed to be at one point or another. Chosen to be in the club or on the team. Chosen to be someone's best friend or girlfriend. Chosen for the reward, or for the job.

The overweight, socially awkward, poorly dressed, insecure little girl living inside of me still remembers what it was like to outwardly appear apathetic but inwardly scream my own name over and over again. I desperately hoped that somehow, through forced telepathy, the team captain would open their mouth and I would hear my name. I was not the most favorable pick for a kickball team; inevitably the choosing pool would dwindle, body by body, until, with only myself and another girl remaining, I would hear, "Okay, I guess I'll take Tanya." Being chosen by default is not the same as being chosen by choice.

To be chosen means that you've been intentionally set apart from others with a purpose in mind; that you are special and different in ways that cause you to have value above others. How hard it can be for us to believe that the God of the universe and Creator of all things has purposefully and intentionally chosen us to accomplish His very important work here upon the earth. The most important work! And yet, it's true. He has chosen **YOU**, Daughter of God, to represent Him here on the earth to others.

He has called you to be "Jesus with skin on." YOU-flavored Jesus. You are the chosen vessel through which He desires to pour His love, encouragement, and kindness into the lives of others in ways that He only can through you. You are one of a kind. No one else has your particular life experiences, gifts, and personality. No one else on this entire earth can shine Jesus into this dark and dying world with the same brilliance and unique magnificence as you can.

You are one of a kind.

You are chosen by Him.

No one else can take your place or

do your job better than you.

Typically an introspective person, twice a year I become especially so. New Year's Day and my birthday have always served as semiannual evaluations for where I think I "should be."

You see, I'm a bit goal-oriented. Other appropriate words might be *focused, driven, passionate,* um... *obsessed.* I carry around with me an invisible measuring stick for my life, determining within my own heart whether I am succeeding in living it to the fullest.

I've come to recognize this trait as a mixed blessing. Innocently bred, it originates from a heart of thankfulness for the life I've been given. Realizing the abundance of the gift, I have never wanted to spend one day wasting it.

Make every day count, reach for the stars, never give up, keep on keepin' on... motivational mottos are fuel for the engine of my soul.

On the other hand, this constant need to evaluate growth toward goals set high has left much room for the enemy to whisper in my ear. A dog with no new tricks, he has often found a foothold in my life with the *should-be's.*

In his accusatory tone, he offers:

"You *should be* further along than you are."

"You *should be* a better wife, mother, Christian, friend."

You *should be* beyond a place where that still bothers you." (When I'm flustered, frustrated, or fearful.)

"You *should be* everything you are not."

How many times have I fallen into that hole and had to dig myself back out?

I *should* have seen that coming!

It is important for both you and me to remember that goals are good, but only as long as they are balanced with truth.

When the enemy comes at me with his *should-be's* these days, I come back at him with some *should-be's* of my own.

I remind him from where the Lord has brought me, and how He has redeemed my life from destruction (Psalm 49:15).

You see, according to statistics:

I *should be* a high school dropout.

I *should be* married to an abusive husband.

I *should be* a rotten mom.

I *should be* an addict.

I *should be* dead.

I *should be* going to hell.

Any time the enemy tries to accuse me of not being where I should be, I now remind him of where I am not because of the abundant love, boundless grace, and endless mercy of my Lord and Savior Jesus Christ.

How about you? Are you familiar with the *should-be's*? Does this phrase threaten to light the fire of low self-worth within your soul?

The most important truth doesn't lie in where you should be at all, but instead, in who God's Word states that you are.

You are a Daughter of the King (1 John 3:2).

You are unconditionally loved and accepted by Him (Ephesians 1:4-6).

You are chosen (1 Peter 2:9).

If we can keep in mind who we are, we will be better prepared not to allow the *should-be's* to wreak havoc in our soul.

Often, the enemy uses the skillful weapon of *should-be's* against us to try to convince us that we are unusable to our Father. I see it disable and dismantle the hearts of women all the time.

If you can't help yourself, how will you ever help anyone else?

If you are still struggling in this area or that, how can you even think that you matter or have purpose?

You are a mess.

Your ducks are not in a row.

That *is* your circus, and those *are* your monkeys.

There is always a never-ending list waiting to remind us of just how unqualified and inadequate we are to do anything of worth and value for the Kingdom of God.

We can have two different responses to this list— we get to choose. We can allow the enemy to use these reminders to bring shame, guilt, and condemnation into our lives, which is not what God would want, according to Romans 8:1. Or, we can simply agree with him and acknowledge those areas where we still fall short. When we acknowledge the areas of weakness the enemy reminds us of, we dismantle his power to use those facts as a weapon against us.

In the very same breath, however, we can choose to highlight the truth that supersedes the facts. Our gracious God continues to use us smack dab in the middle of our mess. Despite our messiest mess. This only demonstrates—to a higher degree—His great love for us. Despite where we are not, our loving Father, knowing exactly where we would be on every moment of our journey with Jesus, has still chosen us to partner with Him to accomplish His will upon the earth (1 Corinthians 3:9).

The knowledge that in and of ourselves we have nothing to offer to others helps us to better embrace the truth that apart from Him we can do nothing (John 15:5). This is the place where our Father wants us to stay: Nestled in His arms, crawling into His lap, resting in His presence, listening for His voice, and reveling in His willingness to lead and guide us in every task He has called us to.

Daughter of God, listen to this good news: The many places you fall short do not disqualify you from being used in amazing ways by your heavenly Father. In fact, to be used by Him was the very reason you were created— it's in your blood. Thankfully, our God specializes in using the most unlikely and unlovely for His grand and marvelous plans.

Chapter Thirteen

> *For we are His workmanship, created in*
> *Christ Jesus for good works, which God prepared*
> *beforehand that we should walk in them.*
>
> **EPHESIANS 2:10**

1 Corinthians 1:27–29 tells us that God chooses the foolish things to confound the wise and the weak things to shame the strong so that we cannot boast before Him. There is no room for boasting about any beautiful way our Father allows us to serve Him because, at the end of the day, we know ourselves all too well. We know that only in and through Him are we able to do anything of value for others or for Him.

Ephesians 2:10 tells us that "...we are His workmanship, created in Christ Jesus for good works, which God prepared beforehand that we should walk in them." He has created you and chosen you to have a relationship with Him and be used by Him to help others know how very much He loves them. However it looks, whatever form it takes, this is the very important job you have been called to do.

> Therefore, if anyone is in Christ, he is a new creation; old things have passed away; behold, all things have become new. Now all things are of God, who has reconciled us to Himself through Jesus Christ, and has given us the ministry of reconciliation, that is, that God was in Christ reconciling the world to Himself, not imputing their trespasses to them, and has committed to us the word of reconciliation. (2 Corinthians 5:17–19)

The ministry of reconciliation—simplified—is to tell everyone you know: God has always loved you. He is not mad at you. He wants a relationship with you. By accepting Jesus Christ as your Savior, you will be adopted as a child of God; it will rock your world in all the right ways!

We are learning what it means to be seen, known, and unconditionally loved by Him. We are learning of the freedom that comes through the gift of our salvation. We are learning what it means to be able to walk in and embrace our identity as a daughter of the King. However, even as we are on our way to a fuller understanding of what it all means, we have the ability and responsibility to share what we do know with others so that they can receive the very same love, freedom, and forgiveness that we have been given the opportunity to know.

It's a big job, an important job, and a job we have been chosen to do.

The last day of school before Christmas break was unlike any other day of the year. Everyone knew that academics were secondary to celebration and that the true focus of our time together was meant for gift exchanges, cookie eating, glittery crafts, and general Christmas festivities.

As a teacher, I was always blessed by that sweet moment when, one by one, I was approached by my students and gingerly handed a Christmas gift. Kneeling down, I made sure to look them in the eye, hug them tight, and thank them wholeheartedly for their thoughtfulness.

One year, one of my first graders, a freckle-faced cutie with long blond hair and a smile that lit up an entire room, offered a confident proclamation with her gift. "Mrs. Glanzman, I know that you are really going to like my gift." "I know that I will," I assured her with a wink. She repeated, with emphasis, "No, I mean you're really going to like it." Her resoluteness stirred my curiosity. With a sideways glance and a sly grin, I asked, "And why do you think that?" She answered, "Because last year, when someone gave it to my mama, she really liked it!"

Over the years, when finances fell on the slimmer side of things, I too became skilled in the art of re-gifting. Truly thankful for the thoughtfulness of the gift giver, I worked hard at determining if anything given to me could possibly be a blessing to someone who I loved and desired to bless. The blessing of the gift given to me was magnified if I could re-gift it to someone else.

Other times, re-gifting came in handy when someone who didn't know me well would gift me with something that just wasn't "me," but I knew would be exactly what someone else would love. Ultimately, the old adage has proven true: It really is more blessed to give than it is to receive, and it really is the thought that counts.

There are few self-proclaimed re-gifters. The social ramifications of the act and its questionable breach of social acceptability lead most to re-gift in secret. The truth remains, however, that sometimes to give what you have been given just makes the most sense.

As children of God, not only is it acceptable for us to re-gift, but it is expected! Matthew 10:8 tells us that we are to freely give as we have freely received. The truth is, unless we give that which we have been given, we are not successfully fulfilling all that the Lord has called us to. In the Kingdom of God, re-gifting is the only way to do things!

In my own life, I have been given so many wonderful gifts from the Lord that I am compelled to share them with others. Anything that I have that is of value to give is only that which has already been given to me by the Father. As I encounter others along this journey of life, I am continually searching within my own reservoir of gifts, asking the Lord, "What is it, Father, that you have placed within me that I can give to them?"

What have you been given by the Father, beautiful Daughter of God? Comfort, encouragement, love, mercy, grace, forgiveness, and even more? Is there someone the Lord has placed within your life who could really use one of those? And better yet, have one of those poured through you in the unique and magnificent light of the way He created you?

Seek the Father and ask Him what He would have you re-gift to someone else.

Chapter Fourteen

> *O Lord my God, I cried out to You, and you healed me.*
> **PSALM 30:2**

Flashback to fifteen years ago. A young wife and mother-to-be, I struggled to bear the weight of the baggage from my past. Traumatic abuse throughout my childhood led to many residual issues that included deep depression, severe anxiety, and bulimia. The combination of obstacles to overcome simply to live a "normal" life left me constantly feeling overwhelmed, distraught, and discouraged.

In the effort to obtain help from the Body of Christ, I shared my testimony many times as a precursor to the questions of, "How can I get better? How can I lead a normal life? How can I overcome?"

More than once, taken aback by what I had shared and in the absence of something of value to say, fellow Christians offered the quick response of, "What doesn't kill you makes you stronger." This offering was almost always served with a heaping dose of either sarcastic humor or serious conviction. Sometimes, the more spiritual variety would tack on, "Well, ya know, God will never give you more than you can handle."

I still remember the type of emotional response these answers would elicit within me. With biting sarcasm fueled by bitterness, I would often respond, "If this is what it takes for me to be strong... I would rather be weak!" Less forgiving in my thoughts regarding God, I would often think that if He felt He hadn't given me more than I could handle, then He simply didn't know me as well as He thought He did.

The truth is that "What doesn't kill you makes you stronger" is a lie. Sometimes—often, in fact—what doesn't kill you can maim, disable, and disfigure you, leaving you limping and broken for the remainder of your days.

You see, it's not *what* happens to you that makes you stronger. Instead, it is God's ability to bring healing, *despite* what has happened to you. In His miraculous way, He is well able to take what the enemy meant for harm within your life, and mine, and use it to bring life to many (Genesis 50:20).

As children of God, we play a crucial part in this redemptive equation. We must *allow* ourselves to be healed. Although the exact journey to be traveled differs for each one, there are similar pit stops that include surrender, forgiveness, and obedience for all. It's in the hope of healing that we find our strength. It is in the knowledge of God's ability to bring healing in the absence of our own ability to make ourselves better that we find that hope. As children of God, we are strong not because of what happens to us, but in spite of what happens to us, because we can be assured that Our God is mighty to save (Zephaniah 3:17).

EVEN YOU

It was an evening of women getting to know one another better. Following the planned ministry and the dinner, we now sat around in our pajamas, almost feeling guilty about the abundance of unfamiliar free time and the handfuls of M&M's we were enjoying. Away from our jobs, husbands, and children for the weekend, it seemed strange, for once, to only be responsible for ourselves.

Conversation started slowly, dripping like a faucet with a leak, beginning in those places we reflexively go to when someone asks us, "How are you?" This question somehow compels us to share about our children's sports teams, our job, and our husband's latest project around the house. With so much going on as women, we often don't have the luxury to consider "how we are." It was as if we all knew we were broaching the unfamiliar borders of relational intimacy, and this caused us to tiptoe rather than run.

As the night progressed, casual conversation transformed into something more. Women exchanged their street clothes for jammies while beginning to shed their emotional defenses and reserve for authenticity and transparency. One by one, each woman began to share her heart. Minutes turned to hours as we realized how much easier it was to get to know each other outside the confines of before and after church. Heartaches, concerns, and fears were shared openly and honestly as others offered love and encouragement.

Eventually, we arrived at the testimonies. Going farther back, "How did you meet your husband" was replaced with, "How did you meet Christ?" It was here that we ran into a bit of an impasse.

Some women shared openly of their coming to the Lord; dramatic stories of rescue, change, and transformation as a result of salvation touched everyone's hearts. Other women, while listening, became obviously uncomfortable and awkwardly silent. As we made our way around the circle, finally landing on one fidgety sister, she looked up only briefly as she said, "I don't really have a testimony."

Apologetically dismissive, she shared that she had known the Lord her whole life. Growing up in a household where her parents were believers, she could not ever remember a time that prayer, church, and the Word of God were not a part of who she was.

It was obvious that she felt this was a less than acceptable offering in the midst of our salvation stories.

I looked at her and gently assured her that of all the testimonies in the room, my heart would be that the testimony of my own daughter would look most like hers.

There was nothing "less" about her testimony at all, and the non-dramatic elements of her salvation could not delete the miraculous beauty of her redemption. Salvation itself is a dramatic event. In a single moment we exchange guilt for grace, bondage for freedom, and a life separated from God to one in which we are never without Him. Whether you accept Him at age 5, 55, or 105, the value is no less significant, amazing, or tremendous.

Whether it is what He saved you from or what He has walked you through, your testimony is powerful and able to be used by God to minister to others.

Chapter Fifteen

> *Now to Him who is able to do exceedingly*
> *abundantly above all that we ask or think,*
> *according to the power that works in us.*
>
> EPHESIANS 3:20

Initially, when I thought of what the right time to leave the house would be, 9:30 am seemed like a reasonable estimation. I spent the morning planning, packing, and preparing. Lugging my baggage and my friend's belated birthday gift to my mommy-wagon, I set them down and began to dig in my purse for my keys. When the one-hand "dig, feel, and grab" method failed me, I realized that my keys were not in my purse after all. I was going to have to go back into the house to find them.

Exhausting my looking abilities, I reluctantly called my husband. I didn't really want to admit to him that I had lost my keys again, but desperate times call for desperate measures. Graciously forgoing all that he could have said, he told me that the last place he had seen them was on the couch under the clean laundry. Well... *naturally*... why hadn't I thought to look there first?

Keys in hand, I ran to the car, jumped in, and began to back down the driveway. Realizing immediately what the dreadful dragging noise was, I slammed on the breaks. Instantly nauseous, I slowly stepped back out of the car and walked around to the rear for damage assessment. Fortunately, I had not backed up with enough speed to force my luggage beneath the vehicle. Instead, I had only pushed it down my gravel driveway, causing it to get scratched and dirty. Unfortunately, the beautifully wrapped gift that was sitting next to the luggage did not fare as well. Grimacing as I got down on my hands and knees, the gravel digging into my skin, I looked into the darkness of the car's underbelly to see what had become of my friend's exquisitely wrapped birthday gift. Disappointment mingled with frustration as I reached underneath and began ripping the once-white tissue paper out from the car parts it was tangled in. The bag that I had spent much time picking out because I wanted just the perfect one was now ripped, dirty, and ruined.

Expecting the worst and holding my breath, I gingerly removed the remaining tissue paper from the bag to check on the gift within. I was both amazed and relieved to find the special piece of framed art unscathed. Somehow, I had managed to back over it at such an angle that although there was much damage to the beautiful wrapping, what was most important had remained intact.

With no time to do anything about it, I called my friend on the way to meet her, explaining what had happened. Later, offering her a birthday gift that looked like it had been, well... run over, we both were able to laugh together. I was so very thankful to see that the state of the wrapping didn't detract from the blessing of the gift at all.

God has placed gifts inside each one of us. Sometimes the circumstances of life can cause us to feel about as beautiful and useful as something that has been run over and has lived to tell about it. We must remember, though, that although the gifts and callings of God are held within our tattered "wrapping," they remain useful for the purpose of bringing Him glory. We cannot become so "wrapped up" in our own weaknesses and shortcomings that we refrain from offering the gifts within us to others.

I love the way this verse is written in the amplified Bible:

> Who comforts (consoles and encourages) us in every trouble (calamity and affliction), so that we may also be able to comfort (console and encourage) those who are in any kind of trouble or distress, with the comfort (consolation and encouragement) with which we ourselves are comforted (consoled and encouraged) by God. (2 Corinthians 1:4 AMP)

Have you ever noticed how a pregnant woman's presence can bring forth a plethora of birth stories from those that have been there and done that? Giving birth is one of those life-changing experiences that absolutely can become forever engraved upon your memory and imprinted upon your heart!

It seems that as each woman shares her story, there is an inner recognition, understanding, and validation that can only come from those whom have been through the same experience. As women and mothers, we offer a level of empathy and discernment to one another that is not provided by anyone who does not have at least one individual in their lives who calls them "Mama."

Have you ever tried to explain to someone who has never given birth what it is like to give birth? I have, and I must say, it is almost an impossible feat. I shared that it hurt more than anything I had ever experienced, and was different from any other kind of hurt.

The closest I could come to describing it was something along the lines of how it might feel to be squeezed like a tube of toothpaste with the cap still on. "Now... doesn't that sound pleasant?"

I will probably never be asked to teach a birthing class, but the point remains: some things just must be experienced to be understood. Simply explaining to someone what all is encompassed in giving birth is impossible.

To not leave the young, wide-eyed, newly expectant mother completely traumatized at that description of giving birth, I also shared that I never regretted it, and even did it a second time. Despite the misery of pregnancy and the pain of being in labor, the payoff was tremendous. As soon as it was over, I was so focused on the value of the gift I had been given that I concluded that what I went through to get her was unquestionably worth it.

Ultimately, it all boiled down to, "Yes, it was hard, but I got through it, and so will you."

I was thinking recently that the experience of carrying a child and giving birth is like walking out the walk of faith as a child of God.

Trying to explain how it is that we walk by faith and not by sight, and how we trust God during seemingly impossible situations is very difficult when talking with someone who has never done it. These are simply actions that must be experienced to be understood.

Believers that have walked the walk and become the tough that got going when the going got tough are those believers that have also experienced the goodness and faithfulness of God, which has sustained them when nothing else could.

In our chaos, we have found peace.

In our mourning, we have been comforted.

In our impossibility, we have found

the God of the impossible.

Christianity is more than the bumper sticker on our car or the highlighting in our Bible; it is the way we have lived, thrived, and overcome in the midst of our life storms. If you have been a Christian for more than two days, you too have had your own storms through which to sail.

Just as more experienced mothers can speak truth and comfort to those beginning the journey that ends at giving birth, we as Christians have a huge responsibility to share what has been birthed within us with other believers.

Even now, can you recall a time when a deeper level of trust was birthed within you through the labor of a challenging time when you had no choice but to trust God? Has patience been birthed within you through an extended period of waiting on God to move? Has peace been birthed within you in a more tangible way through receiving the peace which transcends all understanding in a very difficult circumstance?

Who is it in your life that could be encouraged, and benefit from hearing your "birth story"? Who needs to hear, "Yes, it is hard, but I got through it, and you will too."?

Acts 10:34 shares with us that God does not play favorites—what He is willing to do for one of His children, He is willing to do for all. The testimony of who God has been within your life can be a huge encouragement to someone who is struggling.

Chapter Sixteen

> *Therefore if anyone is in Christ,*
> *he is a new creation; old things have passed away;*
> *behold, all things have become new.*
>
> 2 CORINTHIANS 5:17

Secretariat was the title of the movie. My daughter loves horses, and therefore any movie of an equine nature is guaranteed to make it to the top of her "must-see" list. We even traveled to the theater for this one and made it an official mommy/daughter date.

I didn't have grand expectations, nor did I plan to get much out of it other than some memorable quality time with my horse-loving girl. Mom "brownie points," if you will.

I was very surprised when, from the first scene of this movie, I could sense the Holy Spirit nudging me, revealing spiritual truths to my heart one after the other, overwhelming me with His presence. It was almost as if throughout the entire movie He was sitting right beside me, sharing my popcorn and whispering in my ear.

The focus of the movie was a horse that was the offspring of a champion. As a captive audience, we witnessed the miracle of its birth and the reaction of its owner, Penny. In a moment of pride and quiet awe, the on-screen spectators to this momentous event held their breath while the slippery and unsteady creature struggled to stand on its spindly legs. Penny informs all within hearing distance with certainty, and a defining tone of authority, that they had, indeed, just been witness to the birth of a champion.

Looking at the just-born creature wobbling to and fro, attempting to stand, to walk, there was nothing at that moment that resembled a champion. We could have just been peering through the life window of any regular, everyday horse. But you see, the one to whom this particular horse belonged knew from where it came and where it was destined to go.

As time went on, despite the blood that coursed through its veins, fewer and fewer could recognize this horse as the champion that it was. In order to be considered a proper racehorse, there were specific criteria that had to be met. Repeatedly, the owner was reminded that her horse just didn't "have what it takes." And yet, again and again, we witness Penny firmly believing in what lay within the creature she called her own, taking chance after chance upon what others considered mere foolishness.

The grand conclusion, without ruining the entire movie for you, is that Secretariat accomplished an equestrian feat that very few other horses have, only because one person refused to give up on him.

The world was stunned as they watched a simplistic, foolish housewife lead a horse that defied all odds into the winner's circle. No one with any sense would ever have placed their bets on either one of them.

The movie ended, the theater lights came on, and I remained still, sitting next to my slightly embarrassed daughter, completely overwhelmed by the cinematic production in which we had just partaken. "Mom, it's okay, it was a happy ending..." I wasn't just silently crying but was bawling, overwhelmed with tears as well as by the Holy Spirit, who had just opened the eyes of my heart to truth right there in the movie theater... row four, seat c. He is always so faithful to meet us right where we are at.

Can you see the correlation? When I was born, when you were born, the Lord already knew what our lives would be. And in the same moment that He witnessed us exiting our mother's womb, within His heart resided the cry, "I have just witnessed the birth of a champion!"

In Romans 8:37, we are assured that, "Yet in all these things we are more than conquerors through him who loved us."

God sees us always as winners, overcomers, victors, and champions! No matter what it looks like, no matter what we face, no matter how foolish we may seem to anyone else, when our Heavenly Father sees us, He sees us through champion-colored glasses. He knows that if we refuse to give up, if we continue to "fight the good fight of faith," we will walk before Him as the victor He declares us to be.

There have been many times when no one with any sense would have placed their bets on me. All odds were against me. I didn't "meet the criteria" of a champion, an overcomer, a conqueror. But God never gave up on me. Each time he chose to take another chance on me when, long ago, others would have gotten fed up, would have given up, and would have tossed me aside.

Have you ever felt the same way? Are there things about you that make you feel as though you fall short, don't meet the standard, aren't "good enough," or just don't measure up? Ever feel foolish or weak? Yes... me too.

I encourage you today to ask the Lord to help you borrow His glasses so that you can see yourself in the same way He does.

Daughter of God, embrace the truth that you are chosen today.

PRAYER

Father, thank you that You have chosen me, right where I am, exactly how I am, to help You accomplish Your will here on the earth. Help me to see and use the unique gifts You have placed within to help others better understand Your love for them.

YOU ARE CHOSEN
Questions for Journal & Discussion

1. Have you ever struggled with feeling significant or purposeful in your walk with God and with others? Can you think of places where He has used you right in the midst of your mess?

2. How has God created you uniquely to shine into the lives of others? What does Jesus-flavored YOU look like?

3. With what has the Father gifted you that you could re-gift to others? Can you think of people in your life right now who could benefit from these gifts through you?

4. Is there an area of hurt in your life that has threatened to maim you that still needs healing? If so, are you willing to allow the truth and healing of God to shine into that place?

5. Do you feel that you currently live a life wrapped in grace, or wrapped up in your weaknesses? How can the Father use your weakest places and moments to shine His truth, love, and life into the lives of others?

SECTION FOUR
You Are Seen

*She gave this name to the L*ORD *who spoke to her: "You are the God who sees me," for she said, "I have now seen the One who sees me."*

GENESIS 16:13 (NIV)

Chapter Seventeen

> *For we do not have a High Priest who cannot sympathize with our weaknesses, but was in all points tempted as we are, yet without sin.*
>
> **HEBREWS 4:15**

Have you met Hagar? In Genesis 16:1–16 we are introduced to this woman who, in the care of others, was forced into a position for which she did not ask but then was punished for. Perhaps you can relate? So many daughters of God find themselves in difficult situations due to other's choices or life circumstances. While they would never voluntarily choose those situations, they nevertheless are forced to contend with:

Anger

Addiction

Abuse

Abandonment

Hagar was a slave to Abraham's wife, Sarah. After many, MANY years of trying, Sarah simply was not able to conceive a child with Abraham. Weary, so very weary of being unable to bear a child, she suggested her husband spend some time with her beautiful slave girl Hagar, thinking that they, together, might be more successful at the task.

I can only imagine the dreary and distraught place within Sarah from which this request was born. Her barrenness had been constant torment to her. Longing for a child, to begin a family. Ashamed, disappointed, and frustrated at her own inability to make it happen, she looked for other avenues of opportunity to get the job done. I am so familiar with this need to take control and make things happen.

This was a typical practice of that culture, but it was not God's best for Abraham and Sarah, to whom He had promised a son.

I will make you a great nation; I will bless you
And make your name great;
And you shall be a blessing.
I will bless those who bless you,
And I will curse him that curses you;
And in you all the families of the earth shall be
blessed. (Genesis 12:2–3)

In Genesis 18, Sarah hears of this promise that God has made to her husband.

She laughed

Sarah, examining the reality of her age and season of life, laughed at the thought of now bearing the child for which her heart had always longed.

> Now Abraham and Sarah were old, well advanced in age; and Sarah had passed the age of childbearing. Therefore, Sarah laughed within herself, saying, "After I have grown old, shall I have pleasure, my lord being old also?" (Genesis 18:11–12)

If I close my eyes and listen hard, I can almost hear the tone of her laugh. It wasn't a faith-filled laugh of joy, or delight in hopeful expectation of the fulfillment of the promise. It was laughter filled with sarcastic bitterness and dubious speculation. Her laughter reflected the whisper of her heart that it felt cruel for God to make this type of a promise when all hope had been lost.

Have you ever felt this way, daughter of God, after hearing a promise that the Father has made in His word? Based on the present realities of your life, do you regard it with a heart that cries out,

> *There's no way!*
>
> *It can't happen!*
>
> *All hope is lost!*

I have.

And the Lord said to Abraham, "Why did Sarah laugh, saying, 'Shall I surely bear a child, since I am old?' Is anything too hard for the Lord? At the appointed time I will return to you, according to the time of life, and Sarah shall have a son." (Genesis 18:13–14)

In the past, when reading God's response to Sarah's doubtful heart, I interpreted a tone of frustration and anger. Irritation with Sarah for her lack of faith and lack of belief that God indeed would be faithful to do what He had promised. Now, however, I sense the grief of His own heart when His daughter didn't believe that as a good father, He would keep His word. Good daddies always keep their promises.

I love that, in response to Sarah's lack of faith, God didn't punitively revoke the promise He had made. Knowing all things, He understood exactly why she responded that way.

He had, after all, been there each time she had wept, grieving what she thought she would never have.

He had heard every secret whisper of her heart as she saw other women with children; "Me too, Lord, me too."

He had known all along what she was yet to know; in His timing and provision, the need for a child within her would be met.

God asked a question to which He already knew the answer for the purpose of revealing the content of a hurting heart.

He saw.

He knew.

He understood.

The Lord is gracious and full of compassion,

Slow to anger and great in mercy.

The Lord is good to all,

And His tender mercies are over all His works.

(Psalm 145:8–9)

And yet, even though He understood why Sarah struggled to believe, He still desired for her to believe that He would be faithful to His word. He longed for her to know that when He specifically says He will do something, He will do it. No matter what it looks like, how hard it seems, or how impossible it is for His children to imagine the how of something coming to pass, He, in His amazing and miraculous working, will always keep His promises.

Trusting in God's promises and waiting for them to come to pass can be challenging, but resting in His faithfulness brings peace to our hearts and allows us to wait patiently on His timing.

Chapter Eighteen

> *Come to Me, all you who labor and are*
> *heavy laden, and I will give you rest.*
> MATTHEW 11:28

The temptation to take control is such a sneaky scheme of the enemy. Like the advertisements for prescription medications that offer relief of whatever ails you, taking control can seem like the perfect solution to whatever problem we face. The screen fills with happy people living happy lives, as things are just the way they should be.

When contemplating taking control, we can almost hear the happy music playing in the background as we visualize things going just the way we plan.

We think, *If they'll just do what I say, it will be okay.*

But then, in those same miracle commercials, all

crammed together in a hurried frenzy at the end, is the long list of potential side effects: Nausea, vomiting, migraines... death.

We see a theme throughout God's Word of women who like to be in control. Eve, Miriam, Martha... I can't deny it myself. A victim of a childhood filled with instability and chaos, I have had to work very hard (and am still working very hard), at not being a "control freak." And in line with each woman I mentioned, I have experienced the negative consequences of this weakness come to pass.

There really isn't joy or pleasure in the need to be in control; in fact, it is a place of torment, a behavior that is spawned from and grows in fear.

~ The fear that things will not work out.

~ The fear that things will not be okay.

~ The fear that things will not turn out the way they should.

Often, this fear has found its beginning in experiences when things didn't work out, were not okay, and didn't turn out the way they should. As a result, the need to prevent further and future pain creates an unhealthy coping skill that likes to rear its ugly head anytime there is an opportunity for things to go wrong.

Somewhere along the way, I began to believe that I knew best, and that it was my job to keep bad things from happening.

If things could just go the way I thought they should, then everything would work out okay.

Without a doubt, it is my husband and children who have suffered the most from the consequences of this type of reasoning. As I'm continuing to work on it to this day, they are still patient with me. There was a time when I deceived myself into thinking that taking control was rooted in the kind-hearted care and keeping of others so that they wouldn't experience negative feelings. I was trying to prevent them from being mad, trying to prevent them from being sad, and trying to prevent them from being anything but happy.

Over time, however, the Lord has revealed that, often, the root of control is self-preservative at best and selfish at worst. Each time I try to take control, what I'm really working to prevent are the negative feelings that I will have if someone I care about experiences negative feelings. When other's emotions are anything but "happy," it causes a certain discomfort to rise within me that breeds a fear-based insecurity. I don't like it when others are unhappy because of the way it makes me feel.

~ Sometimes, however, people are unhappy.

~ Sometimes people need to be unhappy.

~ A place of unhappiness can often serve as a catalyst for much-needed change.

~ Trying to manipulate the emotions of others through control often stifles necessary growth opportunities.

Picture the small child who needs to experience the unhappiness of an unpleasant consequence in order to learn the importance of obedience. If we parent in a way that our children never experience unhappiness, we are poorly preparing them for the reality of this world.

Picture the child of God who has run *from* the Father instead of to Him. It is in the desolation and desperation of that place that the desire for His goodness and grace once known is desired again. Picture the prodigal son; dirty, stinky, and hungry, surrounded by pigs....

Understanding the root of the desire to control within my own heart, I've come to a place where, as soon as I recognize the inner turmoil that would want to flip the switch of control, I intentionally refuse to engage.

Once flipped, that switch can prompt the offering of uninvited "wisdom," or cause me to gingerly step in and take action to make things happen or prevent something from happening. Instead, I must willingly choose to keep my mouth shut and my feet still while praying to see when or if the Lord would direct me to act, rather than react out of my own unhealthy emotional response.

Chapter Nineteen

Therefore they shall eat of the fruit of their own way,
and be filled to the full with their own fancies.

PROVERBS 1:31

Although taking control offers a slice of relief in the moment, there can be long-lasting negative consequences for both the one who is controlling and the ones being controlled.

Unfortunately, as is often the case when we do things our own way instead of God's way, Sarah's plan worked, but things got messy.

Once Hagar knew she was pregnant with Abraham's baby, she began to have some *feelings* toward Sarah. Perhaps feelings of jealousy that Sarah would lay claim to the seed within her to which she already had begun to bond. Pride, possibly, that she, as a slave girl, could do something so very significant that her mistress couldn't. She may have been experiencing frustration at the unfairness of her lot in life while at the same time imagining how painful it might be to stand on the sidelines and watch her child be raised as another's.

These feelings caused a shift in their relationship. Women are relational creatures, and Sarah, who didn't appreciate the change, griped to Abraham. Most women are transparent like plastic wrap, and due to the sensitivity of the situation (a perceived tone here and a possible facial expression there), she began to discern the animosity growing in Hagar's heart while Abraham's baby was growing within her womb. Not wanting to get caught up in the mama drama, Abraham reminded Sarah that Hagar was her slave, and she could do whatever she wanted with her.

Genesis 16:6 tells us that Sarah then mistreated Hagar, and as a result, Hagar, baby in belly, fled. It doesn't tell us how Sarah mistreated Hagar, but it must have been significantly severe because a pregnant slave didn't have too many options to care for herself and her yet-to-be-born child. Running away from her source of sustenance was an act of desperation.

So often, when we carry hurt, frustration, and disappointment, it can be hard not to lay all of it at the feet of someone who rubs up against the wounds in our hearts in just the right way. The person who has what we want. The person who takes for granted that which we long for. The person who is walking in the very fullness of what we have ached to walk in.

It just doesn't seem fair.

It's in these moments that the *why's* in our hearts find a voice of their own and scream to lash out at these others. I remember feeling this way from a very young age as I observed the families of friends in my life. I can recall, at nine years old, hearing other children talk about how upset their parents would get with them over certain things... how messy their rooms were, or the C's instead of A's and B's on their report card.

Out of the deep desperation of wanting parents who cared as much, I would lie and say that my mom, too, was upset with me. For her to be upset about these types of things would be a tangible indication that she noticed me. That at least sometimes I was utilizing more of her thoughts and energy than herself and her addiction.

The truth was, she signed my report card when I asked her to without looking at it or commenting on what was shared about my progress. Most of the time, I didn't have a room to keep clean but instead was sleeping on a couch... on a floor... or in the closet of wherever we happened to be that evening.

In adolescence, I would hear others complain about their parents: how obnoxious they were, how controlling, how intrusive. Inwardly, I resented them for their obvious lack of appreciation for what they had. Outwardly, in each family that I was exposed to, I endeavored to make myself a part of it in any way that I could. I would pretend, during family dinners or activities I was permitted to be a part of, that I, too, was a member of their family with parents that were present.

As a young adult, I would hear other young mamas complain about their mothers or mothers-in-law, about family gatherings that were a burden to attend, or about overly intrusive grandparenting styles. With deep sighs, they would gripe about the struggle of how holidays would be celebrated and how they would manage to meet the expectation of all their loved ones. It took great restraint not to feel jealous. Restraint I simply didn't have at the time. What felt like a burden to them had been a longing of my heart. To have people fight over wanting to spend time with me and my littles? I couldn't imagine it.

I can most closely relate to these types of feelings when remembering the journey we took as a family when my thirteen-year-old daughter Brooke was diagnosed with cancer. In our two and a half years of fighting for her life, I remember so many times of battling those horrible feelings:

IT'S NOT FAIR!

They often welled up big within my heart, sometimes to the point of feeling that it would burst. Partaking in social media became a wretched, self-imposed torture as I watched others share through picture posts the wonderful life experiences being had by their healthy, not sick, normal, happy teenagers. First days of school, proms, homecomings, athletic events, vacations... everything I wanted my daughter to be experiencing with a smile on her face and in her soul.

My eyes would bounce between the images on the screen and my so very sick, wasting away, bald daughter sleeping... always sleeping, on the couch in front of me.

It just wasn't fair.

And somehow, all the unfairness I had ever felt was wrapped into those moments, and I was eaten within by jealousy, bitterness, anger, and deep, deep grief.

It was never that I didn't want those wonderful things for the people who surrounded me. It was just that I wanted them for me too, for my daughter. I wanted someone to care.

I wanted someone to SEE me.

Chapter Twenty

> *Every good gift and every perfect gift is from above,*
> *and comes down from the Father of lights, with whom*
> *there is no variation or shadow of turning.*
>
> **JAMES 1:17**

The loss of normalcy in my daughter's life only served to remind me of the lack of normalcy I had experienced in my own. You see, I had determined from the time she was introduced into the world that *I was going to make sure* that she had the childhood I'd never had. That she would never experience the depth of pain and suffering I had endured. That she would have the picture-perfect childhood I had lacked. It was a mission within me to provide her with the joy, peace, and innocence I'd never been given the opportunity to know. And then, in one conversation, one X-ray, one diagnosis...

...hello, pediatric cancer, meet mama control freak. All at once, it felt as though my ability to control the quality of her childhood was dismissed and forfeited, and instead, was completely out of my control.

And in this, I was like Hagar. Hagar fled, and in Genesis 16, God's Word tells us that she ended up at a spring of water in the wilderness. I can imagine she was a hot mess, hormones raging, a waddling fit of emotion. In anger and fear, she ran... have you ever seen a pregnant woman run? It's not pretty.

She ran into the wilderness, thinking only of getting as far away as she could from the abuse she had endured. I can imagine her dirty, sweaty, and with a tear-stained face, finally collapsing next to a spring to get some water for her parched throat. And right there, in the very midst of her mess, God saw her and sent an angel to her.

I'm no Bible scholar, but I'm certain slaves weren't supposed to run away from their masters. And yet, smack dab in the middle of Hagar's undeniable disobedience, in His love, grace, and mercy, the Lord wanted her to know three things:

He saw her.

He loved her.

He was going to help her.

The angel encouraged her and told her to return to Sarah. In Genesis 16:11, the angel spoke these words to her: "Behold, you are with child, and you shall bear a son.

You shall call his name Ishmael, because the Lord has heard your affliction." It was then that Hagar realized that God had seen her. God's Word states in verse 13 that she called the name of the Lord who spoke to her "a God of seeing."

I believe this was more than simply an angelic directive for Hagar to return to Sarah. All at once, the Father, through the angel He sent, let this hurting and fearful daughter know that He saw her. He was aware of her situation, and He was going to provide the strength and courage she needed to move forward as He led. At His word, peace ruled in her heart, enabling her to return to the same dismal situation that had caused her to flee in the first place.

She knew that He saw her, and it gave her courage.

She knew that He saw her, and it gave her hope.

She knew that He saw her, and that she was not alone.

Sometimes those moments where we know God has seen us happen in big ways, like the appearance of an angel in the wilderness. Sometimes they are a bit less grandiose, yet no less significant.

In autumn of 2013, my daughter, Brooke, was in the fifteenth month of the thirty months required for the treatment protocol for T-cell lymphoblastic lymphoma. Fifteen months of difficult chemotherapy, clinic visits, and long car rides to the hospital several times a week.

Being halfway through this difficult season offered our hearts little reprieve due to the first half of the treatment being so tremendously difficult. In fact, we were probably more stouthearted prior to the beginning of treatment, before we really knew the difficulty of the journey ahead. The awareness of still having so much ahead of us was overwhelming. And yet, what choice did we have but to keep moving forward?

Much of that season is a blur. Our life revolved around helping Brooke survive the very treatment that was intended to save her life. It was a blending of monotonous, difficult days sprinkled with the shock of tremendously heart-wrenching moments. It was in the midst of such difficulty, however, that the moments of God's redemptive love, grace, and mercy shone.

One day in the autumn of 2013 is particularly memorable. I've always loved autumn. The beauty of the transition between the seasons serves as a reminder to me of the love and generous kindness God has for us. I've pondered often the concept that all the leaves *could have been* just a dull grey, but instead, in the awe-inspiring way that He does, He provides breathtaking beauty for us to enjoy. The season of autumn has always felt like a gift to me.

In the gift of autumn, the Lord breathes fresh life into my soul. Pumpkins, apples, the color scheme of orange, red, brown, and yellow... these things make my heart smile BIG. But this particular year, I was simply too weary and worn down by the circumstances of life to notice the splendidness of the season. The joy found in the little everyday things had been lost and buried beneath the enormous pile of struggle just to get from morning to night with my very sick little girl.

On this day, as I drove home from the hospital, I was particularly tired and emotional. It had been a spinal tap day. Brooke was required to get spinal taps regularly throughout treatment to ensure that her spinal fluid remained disease-free. Spinal tap days were long, exhausting days. Being one of the older kids in the pediatric oncology clinic, she always had to wait for the younger patients, who also needed this procedure, before she was served. She wasn't allowed to eat before the procedure, which sometimes meant no food for most of the day. Her already nauseous stomach struggled with these parameters. The long, difficult days spent waiting in the pediatric oncology clinic were draining for both of us.

She slept as I drove home. There was no particular trigger for my quietly falling tears; they were motivated by pure exhaustion. I've found that nothing requires more energy than watching someone you love suffer, without the ability to do anything to make it all better.

Eyes forward, my mind strayed to a million different places. I was surprised when I came upon the entrance to our neighborhood, the forty-five-minute driving time from the hospital seeming to vanish within my thoughts.

Approaching our home, I caught a splash of color. Turning my head to take it in fully, I realized that someone had placed six beautiful chrysanthemums along the length of my front porch. Mums have always been one of my favorite parts of the celebration of autumn. That year, however, finances, time, and lack of energy had prevented me from decorating at all.

In that moment, I knew God saw me.

Quietly turning the car off, I just sat, closed my eyes, and allowed His gracious love to envelop me. I didn't know who He had used to place the mums. What I did know, however, is that they could not have known how this act of kindness would touch the very depths of my soul. In that seemingly simple gift of grace from my Heavenly Father, that young, tired, struggling mama that was me knew that...

He saw her, and it gave her courage.

He saw her, and it gave her hope.

He saw her, and that she was not alone.

For someone else in that same situation, flowers placed on their porch might not have meant to them what it meant to me in that moment. For me, it meant that my Father SAW me. And not only did He see me, but He was using a beautiful form of life that I loved to bring me life. It was a personalized presentation of love and encouragement.

~ Reminding me that the season that we were in was just a season.

~ Reminding me that He was still there, offering the strength and courage we needed to get through.

~ Reminding me that even though life was very hard, He had not forgotten about me.

God sees you, Daughter of God, right in the midst of the mess that you are in.

Right in the midst of the stress, struggle, and storm, He sees you, He loves you, He is for you, and He is ever working on your behalf to help you have the life He has created you to live.

Chapter Twenty-One

> *Look at the birds of the air, for they neither sow nor reap nor gather into barns; yet your heavenly Father feeds them. Are you not of more value than they?*
>
> MATTHEW 6:26

Nothing that deals with the care and keeping of you escapes Him. Different than others, He is never indifferent to your pain. No matter how insignificant you may feel, to Him, you matter.

These truths, Daughter of the King, are the very ones that the enemy of your soul would like to convince you are not true. He would like nothing more than for you to examine the evidence of your life's circumstances and arrive at the conclusion that your creator and the very lover of your soul doesn't really care about you at all.

Through sly, slithering subtleties and twisted, tainted taunts, he schemes with the motive to deceive.

An uncreative enemy, he has no new tricks. From the beginning, in Genesis 3:1-3, we are able to see that the fall of man began in his question to Eve:

"Did God really say...?"

Eve knew exactly what God had said, and she recounted it to the slithering Satan. Not quick to give up, he exchanged the tactic of trying to get her to doubt what God had said to the tactic of tempting her to doubt that what He had said was true.

"You certainly won't die!"

The enemy is a liar. Jesus says,

He was a murderer from the beginning, and does not stand in truth, because there is no truth in him. When he speaks a lie, he speaks from his own resources, for he is a liar and the father of it. (John 8:44)

Who do you think he is speaking to, Daughter of God? Has he ever lied to you? Tried to convince you that you don't really matter, and that God doesn't really care?

The evidence in the hearts of women that I encounter in each place of my life on a daily basis urges me to align with the apostle Paul when he said,

But I am afraid that just as Eve was deceived by the serpent's cunning, your minds may somehow be led astray from your sincere and pure devotion to Christ. (2 Corinthians 11:3 NIV)

In the inability to recognize the lies of Satan that have infiltrated their hearts, minds, and souls, women are deceived into believing things about their Heavenly Father that are simply not true. These fabrications of the enemy absolutely do not line up with the truth about who God is and has so graciously, time and again, affirmed Himself to be in His Words of life to us.

For this very reason, it is not only necessary but vital, Daughter of God, to intentionally and purposefully filter every single thought that finds its way into your mind through the truth of God's Word. It is our most effective weapon.

> Finally, my brethren, be strong in the Lord and in the power of His might. Put on the whole armor of God, that you may be able to stand against the wiles of the devil. For we do not wrestle against flesh and blood, but against principalities, against powers, against the rulers of the darkness of this age, against spiritual hosts of wickedness in the heavenly places. Therefore take up the whole armor of God, that you may be able to withstand in the evil day, and having done all, to stand.

> Stand therefore, having girded your waist with truth, having put on the breastplate of righteousness, and having shod your feet with the preparation of the gospel of peace; above

all, taking the shield of faith with which you will be able to quench all the fiery darts of the wicked one. And take the helmet of salvation, and the sword of the Spirit, which is the word of God. (Ephesians 6:10–17)

Our spiritual battle is one in which our God has faithfully provided to us an arsenal of tools with which to fight. We must choose to put on, pick up, and take hold of the truths within His Word as He instructs.

Hide them in our hearts.

Speak them from our lips.

Apply them to our lives.

It is our primary battle strategy against the very one who comes, as it states in John 10:10, to steal, to kill, and to destroy.

In Matthew 4:1–11, Jesus, our example in all things, shows us exactly what this looks like.

Three different times Satan tried to tempt Christ. Three different times, in response to the offered temptation, Jesus responded with the Word.

Satan: "If you are the Son of God, command that these stones become bread."

Jesus: "It is written, 'Man shall not live by bread alone, but by every word that proceeds from the mouth of God.'"

Satan: "If you are the Son of God, throw yourself down. For it is written: 'He shall give His angels charge over you,' and, 'In their hands they shall bear you up, lest you dash your foot against a stone.' "

Jesus: "It is written again, 'You shall not tempt the Lord your God.' "

Satan: "All these things I will give You if you will fall down and worship me."

Jesus: "Away with you, Satan! For it is written, 'You shall worship the Lord your God, and Him only shall you serve.' "

Again, Satan has no new tricks.

In his first attempt to tempt, challenging the identity of Christ, he began his statement to Jesus with, "If you are the Son of God..."

In his second attempt, Satan schemed to use the very Word that was the weapon being used against him by Jesus by twisting the truth in a way that would offer only a partial truth.

In his third attempt, Satan appealed to the flesh rather than the spirit of Christ.

Each time, Jesus overcame the temptation that Satan offered with the most powerful weapon He had. The truth of God's Word poured out of Him.

These are the very same schemes with which the enemy comes at you, Daughter of God.

He attacks your identity.

He twists the truth.

He appeals to your flesh rather than your spirit.

I am thankful that Jesus demonstrated to us exactly

how to use the weapon of the Word when the enemy of our soul comes knocking at the door of our own hearts.

Know who you are, daughter of God.

Know the truth that will set you free.

Know the benefit of embracing what God says is best.

When we truly understand what God's Word says about who He is and who we are, and when those truths serve as the firm and secure foundation upon which we stand, the enemy's lies are rendered powerless against us. "You shall know the truth, and the truth shall make you free" (John 8:32).

Daughter of God,

He sees you,

He knows you,

He loves you.

As His daughter, you will never be forsaken or forgotten. Whatever battle, struggle, or storm you are in the midst of today, His Word is the weapon He has given so that you not only fight valiantly but overcome completely.

Daughter of God, begin to embrace the truth today that your Heavenly Father sees you and has provided you with His Word, enabling you to overcome in every situation you face.

PRAYER

Father, thank You that You see me and that You care. Because I know You see me, I can be confident that there is no part of my life You are not intimately acquainted with. Thank you that You are always working on my behalf to help me be the overcomer You have called me to be.

YOU ARE SEEN
Questions for Journal & Discussion

---

1. Can you recall a situation in which you wondered if God actually saw you? In what way, big or small, did He remind you in the midst of it that He was right there with you?

2. Is there a specific area or areas within your life where you have lost hope that the promise of God could come to pass? Moving forward, what truth will you stand upon?

3. Do you now struggle, or have you ever struggled, with control? If so, in what specific area can you choose to begin letting go of control?

4. Are you able to identify any lies that you have accepted as truth that do not align with the truth of God's Word? If so, what are they, and what truth of God can you use as a weapon to overcome them?

5. In what ways can you intentionally and purposefully make God's Word a priority in your life?

SECTION FIVE
You Are Led

I sought the LORD, and He heard me,
and delivered me from all my fears.

PSALM 34:4

Chapter Twenty-Two

> *I sought the Lord, and He heard me,*
> *and delivered me from all my fears.*
>
> **PSALM 34:4**

Too many women of God have a distorted idea of who He is and who He says they are and struggle with the concept that their Heavenly Father will actually lead them. Not just that He can, but that He will. The inevitable result of this struggle is fear. Paralyzing fear that keeps them stuck in a place they don't want to be yet don't know how to escape from.

Have you ever experienced this fear, Daughter of God?

- Fear that you needed His wisdom, and He would withhold it?

- Fear that you wouldn't be able to hear His voice?

◡ Fear that you were on your own?

Several misconceptions lead to this fear:

~ I can't hear Him; He doesn't talk to me.

~ It's my fault I'm in this mess; I can't expect Him to get me out.

~ I've not done "all the things" I should have; I don't deserve His help in this.

~ God is too busy to help with this; other people have bigger problems.

~ He doesn't really care about me or I wouldn't be in this situation to begin with.

Many times, these misconceptions lead women to not ask for help from their heavenly Father because ultimately, they believe it's a pointless endeavor.

Filtering every thought through the truth found in God's Word helps us battle and overcome these truth distortions. In His Word, God makes it clear, time and again, that not only is He willing to lead and guide us on our journey through life, but as our kind and loving Father, He desires to do so.

He promises us that...

If any of you lacks wisdom, let him ask of God, who gives to all liberally and without reproach, and it will be given to him. But let him ask in faith, with no doubting, for he who doubts is

like a wave at sea driven and tossed by the wind.
(James 1:5–6)

I love that the quantifiers God places on this promise are very specific and not what you might think. He didn't say IF you...

~ Read your Bible every day this week

~ Haven't missed church lately

~ Didn't do anything to get yourself in this mess

That then He would be faithful to lead you with His wisdom. Nope. There is only one quantifier to receive this particular promise of God.

If you lack wisdom, ask in faith.

No matter the situation in which you find yourself and regardless of how you got there, Daughter of God, His Word is still sure.

He deeply desires to lead you.

He has all the answers you need.

He wants and waits for you to ask.

Exchanging our own wisdom for His as we run this race set before us is vital to a life well-lived. We are limited within the realms of our own humanity, and our self-led decision-making skills too often are built upon the weak foundations of our flesh:

- ~ Fear

- ~ Pride

- ~ Selfishness

- ~ Ambition

- ~ Greed

There is a way that seems right to a man, but its
end is the way of death. (Proverbs 14:12)

We cannot trust in ourselves alone, ladies; it's just
not smart. Our Father is more than willing to provide the
wisdom we need to live our very best life on this earth.
When we fail to access this wisdom, we are short-changing
both ourselves and others. It's not what we should want,
and it's certainly not what He wants for us.

Daughter of God, there is a better way.

Trust in the LORD with all your heart,
And lean not on your own understanding;
In all your ways acknowledge Him,
And He shall direct your paths. (Proverbs 3:5–6)

He *shall* direct your paths.
The paths of your...
> *Marriage, Mothering, and Ministry.*

The paths of your...
> *Heartache, Hurt, and Healing.*

The paths of your...
> *Character, Calling, and Career.*

All of your paths.

This is what is said about the goodness of God's wisdom within His Word:

> Length of days is in her right hand,
> In her left hand riches and honor.
> Her ways are ways of pleasantness,
> And all her paths are peace.
> She is a tree of life to those who take hold of her,
> And happy are all who retain her.
> (Proverbs 3:16–18)

All of us need more of these things in our lives.

Chapter Twenty-Three

> *Do not be anxious about anything, but in every*
> *situation, by prayer and petition, with thanksgiving,*
> *present your requests to God. And the peace of God,*
> *which transcends all understanding, will guard your*
> *hearts and minds in Christ Jesus.*
>
> **PHILIPPIANS 4:6-7 (NIV)**

When we understand the importance of asking for God's wisdom and yield to His desire to lead us, we are then able to move forward in these truths, taking every opportunity to ask for and receive these amazing gifts of grace in every area of our lives.

Isn't it just like our God to give us a twofer? When we humble ourselves, seek His face, and ask for His wisdom in all situations, not only does He give us His wisdom, but He provides His peace as well.

Peace that transcends all understanding when you feel overwhelmed, when it seems hopeless, and when it's just too much.

Can you recall a time, Daughter of God, when you have experienced this very peace? I have, and for me, it's a further demonstration of His abundant faithfulness in the face of situations that are just too big for me to handle in my own strength.

The dynamic between leader and follower depends a great deal on the level of intimacy between them. The more you know someone—their mannerisms, their tone, and the ways they communicate—the easier it is to follow them well. The more time you spend with your heavenly Father, Daughter of God, the more easily you will be led by Him.

Here are three of the ways that God leads us as His children:

~ Through the truth found in His Word

~ Through an inner leading

~ Through His wisdom poured through others

In 2 Chronicles 20, we see how King Jehoshaphat was led by God. He was the king of Judah and discovered that enemies were on their way to attack his land and his people. Jehoshaphat, being the man of God that he was, did what made the most sense to him...

He set himself to seek the Lord.

In his prayer, he reminded himself of who his God was and what his God had done. He then stated what he and his people would do as they were standing and trusting God for His help, fully expecting that He would both hear and save them.

O Lord God of our fathers, are You not God in heaven, and do You not rule over all the kingdoms of the nations, and in Your hand is there not power and might, so that no one is able to withstand You?

Are You not our God, who drove out the inhabitants of this land before Your people Israel, and gave it to the descendants of Abraham, Your friend forever?

And they dwell in it, and have built You a sanctuary in it for Your name, saying,

"If disaster comes upon us—sword, judgment, pestilence or famine—we will stand before this temple and in Your presence (for Your Name is in the temple), and cry out to You in our affliction, and You will hear and save." (2 Chronicles 20:6–9)

Jehoshaphat led his people in this prayer, ending with,

For we have no power against this great multitude that is coming against us; nor do we know what to do, but our eyes are on You." (2 Chronicles 20:12)

And then, through someone in the crowd, the Lord spoke and told Jehoshaphat *exactly* what to do. The Lord reminded them not to be afraid because the battle was not theirs, but His! And I love what God says in verse 17:

"You will not need to fight in this battle. Position
yourselves, stand still and see the salvation of the
Lord, who is with you, O Judah and Jerusalem!"
Do not fear or be dismayed: tomorrow go out
against them, for the LORD is with you.

In response, Jehoshaphat and all his people
worshipped the Lord.

The next day, they faced their enemy. The weapon
they fought with was the praise and worship for their
living God arising from their hearts. And just as God had
said, their enemy was defeated.

> *"Jesus Christ is the same yesterday*
> *and today and forever"*
> **HEBREWS 13:8 (NIV)**

This is one of my favorite things about our Lord! We
can know what to expect from Him because His character
is stable, fixed, and sure. What He has done is what He
will be faithful to do. The only exception to this is when
He has said explicitly within His Word that He will not do
a certain thing again.

He is so trustworthy in this way. Unlike fickle
human beings whose decisions can be influenced by
their mood, motivation, or manic moments, every
decision He makes is based only on His goodness and
is meant only for our good.

Therefore, Daughter of God, you can know beyond a shadow of a doubt that because He is the God who has led His children, He is and will continue to be the God who leads His children.

You, Daughter of God, are His child.

Chapter Twenty-Four

Teach me to do Your will, for You are my God;
Your Spirit is good. Lead me in the land of uprightness.

PSALM 143:10

In order to be led, it is important that we properly position ourselves for that to happen. We must, like Jehoshaphat, set ourselves to seek the Lord. God is not a puppet-master but a perfect Father. He never forces His will upon us, but instead, is a constant source of help and wisdom to those who seek Him. We must desire to be led, and honestly, for many that does not come naturally.

In truth, it's not entirely our fault. From the time we are very young, great praise is given for even small, self-accomplished feats.

"Look at you; you did it all by yourself!"

We live in a society that strongly promotes independence, and our culture values being able to accomplish and succeed on our own. The most glory is given to the one who can get the job done, and the less help needed along the way, the louder the cheers.

This fact, in combination with our prideful human flesh, results in us struggling with dependence.

We want to be able to have it all together.

We feel weak when we need to ask for help.

We don't want to have to rely on others.

It can be such a struggle to reach out in authenticity and vulnerability and admit that we can't do it alone. To do so requires honesty in our ugliness and admittance of our weakness, a choice that comes with great risk.

Hello, aisle of bestseller "self-help" books at the book store! If we can just read a book and fix whatever our problem is, we are saved the trouble of ever needing help from anyone—including God.

As a counselor, I witness this struggle up close and personal on a regular basis. Those who sit on my office couch the first few times seem to do so with disappointment that they needed to come at all. In their eyes, counseling is a tangible token of their failure to be able to fix themselves. Many believe this is proof that they are inadequate, insufficient, and a failure.

Obvious anxiety reveals itself in those first sessions as they share what brought them to counseling. While sharing, they either avoid eye contact entirely or fiercely search my expression for the judgment, rejection, or disgust they expect to find.

I'm thankful that I personally have experienced those same feelings while sitting on someone else's couch. I understand first-hand how difficult it is to walk into a stranger's office and hand over the contents of my heart. Empathetic to that all-too-familiar discomfort of feeling weak, I always do my best to assure each one that they are in a safe place and that those things they are so afraid of finding as they share their story won't be found.

As an adult, I put off going to counseling for many years. I think back now at how helpful it could have been in so very many places. How much lighter my load would have been had I been able to unpack some of my baggage sooner as I struggled as an adult child of an addict, within my marriage, with parenting, and in relationships of every variety.

Had I experienced a childhood that included all of the things I should have had—love, stability, security, and safety, I imagine I wouldn't have had the depth of struggles that I did. So much of what people struggle with as adults truly are the results of unhealed wounds from their past, when they didn't get what they truly needed along the way. Thought and behavior patterns developed during the unhealthy, dysfunctional situations in which they were immersed, often by no choice of their own.

People, with their unique blend of personalities and character traits, are affected differently by the difficult circumstances they encounter. For those who have learned that relying upon others isn't a safe or wise option, self-sufficiency becomes one of their most frequently utilized coping skills.

Chapter Twenty-Five

> *By pride comes nothing but strife,*
> *but with the well-advised is wisdom.*
>
> **PROVERBS 13:10**

It took two years for me to begin counseling after my mother died. At any prior suggestion of it, I had responded with a prideful scoff and felt emotionally slapped as if it were an insult. The unhealthy way in which I was living my life prompted that gentle offering from those who cared for me deeply but saw the unhealthy relational spin cycle in which I was stuck. Exhausting their own efforts to get me unstuck, they had absolutely no idea of how to help me move forward.

I didn't finally go to counseling because I wanted to. I went reluctantly, resentfully, as the result of an ultimatum. A dear friend and mentor, one of the many I had adopted in my heart as a surrogate mother, had recognized the toxic and unhealthy relational traits that characterized the way I related to her.

She felt the pressure of my expectations and was concerned that when she disappointed me, my hurt and disappointment from the unresolved issues with my birth mother would be offered to her. She knew it would hurt us both. She told me that if I didn't go to counseling, she would not be able to continue to be in relationship with me. The truth she spoke resounded within my soul.

This ultimatum, more than anything, made me angry. I considered the option of just never talking to her again, the perceived threat of abandonment and rejection eliciting within me that kick-bucket response of doing that to her before she could do it to me. At least–in my mind–if she was going to abandon me anyway, I could be in control of the pain rather than being a victim of it. I vacillated between the pools of shame and self-pity, embarrassed by my apparent deficiencies in the places she had lovingly called out. I didn't like how I acted; I just didn't know how to be any different.

And it wasn't that I hadn't tried. Prayer services, altar calls, Bible studies, pastoral counseling... you name it, I tried it. I had exhausted the venues I knew of and had been comfortable with and was still, in many places, just as "stuck" as ever. It wasn't that I wasn't aware that there was something wrong, but my stubborn pride convinced me that because I was in *ministry*, I shouldn't need to go to a professional counselor. I was convinced that because I spoke truth into the hearts of women and wrote devotionals about the goodness of God, I should only receive counsel from within the walls of the church. Where did I even get that from? Not from Jesus, that's for *sure*. I felt abhorrence with myself that I couldn't get my act together, angry that I needed help to be better, and ashamed that I had such weakness that I couldn't hide.

This independent, self-sufficient control freak simply couldn't overcome the deep wounds within that resulted in the needy behaviors she displayed. It left me with a choice to make. Would I trust the truth that came through this woman I believed loved both my Lord and me? Would I allow my pride to determine my course, or would I yield to what I could not deny the Lord was leading me to and had, in fact, been leading me to for a long time?

His wisdom poured through her was confirmation of the truth He had already spoken to me. As if my heart was the homing station of truth, this particular bit of wisdom undoubtedly landed right where it belonged. In fact, this has been an ongoing identifier of the times when God uses others to speak His truth into my heart. Each time, the truth spoken aligns with the truth of God's Word, and there is an undeniable knowing in my spirit. I sense an identification, acceptance, and confirmation of that which has been spoken as truth... whether I like it or not.

Those first months of counseling were excruciating. Thank you, Jesus, for the strong woman of God who sat across from me and saw me through His eyes.

I laugh now as I remember that first session. After matter-of-factly pouring out the "highlights" of my complicated and extensive history and what had led me to seek help now, I pointedly asked her, in a dueling tone of doubtful challenge, "So, do you think you can help me?" I was harsh and hard as I sized her up with a glare that screamed a lack of confidence in her ability to offer anything of value to my life.

She responded, "I believe God can help you, and I will do my best to walk beside you on the journey." Taken off guard by her response—and a little disappointed with the solidness of her answer—I responded in a defeated tone, "Well then, how long is this going to take?"

It would have been *so much* easier if she had said, "No, I'm so sorry, you are just way too messed up; there is no help for you." That would have been the answer that validated within me what I already believed was true.

Angry at God that He and I couldn't just fix this "little" problem together, I was bitter and resentful that this was the humiliating path on which He had led me. *So very frustrated* that I needed to go to counseling for help. What had I done or was I doing wrong, I wondered, to prevent me from being able to just go straight to the source rather than have to have His wisdom filtered through a human being?

I had trust issues that were serious, severe, and strong.

Today, on the other side of healing, I'm so thankful

that He led me, even through the ultimatum of another, to go to counseling. What I learned on that journey was that counseling was the venue through which the Lord chose to bring healing into my heart, because a huge part of what was wrong with my heart was its unwillingness to trust another human being.

God knew what I needed, more and better than I did, and He led me to it.

He never, however, removed my ability to choose. He didn't force me to go. I was reminded of that choice time and time again when it was hard. It was so hard! I had to choose to face the years of woundedness, rejection, abuse, and abandonment that I had been trying, for the entirety of my adult life, to get away from and forget.

Every single time I pulled into that parking lot, I was reminded that I was still suffering the negative effects of all that had been done to me or had not been done for me. Every single time, without fail, it brought up feelings of anger, bitterness, and deep-seated grief... until one day, it didn't.

Eventually, after a lot of hard work (make no mistake, Daughter of God, healing can be such very hard work), I was able to reframe the gift of counseling into just that... a gift. I became thankful for each session and the opportunity to work through, with my counselor and my Lord, those wounded places that needed His healing.

To this day, there is a stigma that accompanies going to counseling. A misconception that it is a tool utilized only by the weak... the deficient... the ones that are "crazy." Now, as a licensed professional counselor, I can say with utmost certainty that the very opposite is true. The men and women that walk into my office are brave enough to be honest about their weak places, courageous enough to hear hard truth and embrace it as their own, and strong enough to embark on a journey that promises not only pain but also healing.

God longs to lead you, Daughter of God.

Will you choose to follow?

Following is no easy task. It requires trust, dependence, and an acknowledgment that our Heavenly Father not only knows us but also knows what is best for us. Even when it makes absolutely no sense to us.

Chapter Twenty-Six

> *It is better to trust in the* LORD
> *than to put confidence in man.*
> **PSALM 118:8**

When the time arrived for me to graduate from high school and go to college, I was ready. Nothing sounded better to me than to be done with childhood and move into this undeniably more independent season of life.

No one to tell me what to do or where to go... no one to be the boss of me but me.

Of all the universities from which to choose, the one that found its way into my heart was a very small conservative Christian college with a student population of just over 2,000.

The campus was stunning, the dorms were unintegrated, the curfew was 9:00 pm, and weekly chapel attendance was required. Everything about this school represented that which was safe, stable, and secure. This, I had decided, was where I wanted to be. I longed for safe, stable, and secure.

Looking back, I realize that the primary reason I chose this school was because I so desperately wanted to be the breed of student who would attend this variety of university. I was now, as a college student, striving to steal back some of the innocence of life that had been stolen from me.

Even though I couldn't afford it, off to this picture-perfect school I went. It didn't take long for me to realize that I was "spot on" in my college student profiling. From my roommate to my dorm mates, I was surrounded by peers who had, for the most part, grown up in homes that were safe, stable, and secure.

These were kids whose parents sent them care packages and spending money. These were kids who didn't have to work. These were kids who called home several times a week to touch base with those they had left behind.

And there, surrounded by the thousands, I again felt all alone. Isn't it amazing how alone we can feel, surrounded by so many?

In our home.

At our job.

Within the walls of our church.

Simply being around these people didn't make me one of them. It became apparent very quickly that the baggage on the luggage cart of my heart seemed bigger, heavier, and uglier than the baggage on theirs.

And yet, as much as I wanted to be like them, I *didn't* want to.

Their dependence on their parents baffled me. I remember one night, lying on my bunk in my dorm room "studying" while actively eavesdropping on my roommate's conversation with her parents. I can still remember the feeling that rose up within me when I heard her ask permission to go out on a date with a young man of whom she was quite fond.

She was obviously happy with her parent-given permission to move forward with her plans. Confusion— and if I'm honest, disgust—kept me from rejoicing with her and prompted my curiosity.

"Why did you ask their permission? If you had just done what you wanted to do, they would have never known. Why would you willingly give them the opportunity to say 'No' to you when you could have just done what you wanted to do?"

As baffled by my question as I was by her behavior, she defensively explained to me that she loved and trusted her parents and knew her parents loved her. In her experience, they knew best, and it was important to her that she have their blessing. She embodied respect and Godly submission to the authority figures in her life.

What this sweet young woman saw as submission, I simply saw as control. In my world, control had been anything but safe, authority figures had been anything but trustworthy, and in response, my life's anthem had become, "You're not the boss of me; don't tell me what to do."

This being only one of the many areas in which we were very different, she had no idea how to relate to me, and our roommate relationship didn't last longer than the semester. Truth be told, at that time in my life, I'm sure I was not the roommate her parents would have chosen for her and was more likely the kind of girl they had always warned her to stay away from.

I'm not sure if she'll ever read this, but now might be a good time to say to her, "Dear roomie, I'm sorry I read your journal when you were out. That was wrong; please forgive me. Thank you, however, for your written expression of concern over my eternal salvation. I appreciate that you cared. You can rest assured; I was really saved then, and I am really saved now. Looking forward to hanging out with you and Jesus one day!"

I had learned early on that others were not to be trusted, especially those who were in charge of me. Can we say, "authority issues"?

Being controlled in all the wrong ways by all the wrong people had distorted my ability to see submission as anything but a four-letter word that had ten letters.

This wasn't the only place I felt like a duck among swans. While they were busy with Bible study, I was busy sneaking out of the dorm to visit my soldier boyfriend at the military installation (side note: the man I've now been married to for twenty-three years).

Too many times I didn't make the very curfew that had initially made me feel safe and cared for, and that eventually caught up with me. When I needed my transcript in order to transfer to another school, I had a $200.00 fine to pay due to curfew violations.

Authority issues. They caused a lot of problems for me. From teachers to bosses and from church leaders to my husband–and, ultimately, to my Lord–it's been a tremendously difficult and painful process to learn to have a heart of submission.

Chapter Twenty-Seven

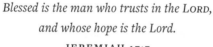

> *Blessed is the man who trusts in the* Lord,
> *and whose hope is the Lord.*
>
> **JEREMIAH 17:7**

How about you, Daughter of God? Do you have any issues with submission? Trouble trusting authority? Difficulty deferring what you think is best in order to rest?

Submission requires trust:

~ *Trust that the person in charge of me is for me.*

~ *Trust that what they are directing me to do is really in my best interest and not just theirs.*

~ *Trust that the person in charge of me is trustworthy.*

These were all things I had to learn about my Heavenly Father. In order to trust Him, it was vital that a few foundational things be established within my heart.

His heart is for me.

My best interest is always what is in the center of His heart.

He is trustworthy.

So much of our ability to trust the Father depends upon us knowing His character. This, as well as understanding His past performance and seeing life from His viewpoint, facilitates our ability to trust Him.

Getting to know Him and learning to trust Him was a journey of a thousand steps. I'm still on this journey, in fact, and it has taken me to places I could never have imagined. The truth found in His Word has undeniably been my tour guide for this journey.

Who God reveals Himself to be in His Word is our best source for knowing who He is. He is His Word.

In the beginning was the Word, and the Word was with God, and the Word was God. (John 1:1)

For a girl with trust issues, this was an important truth to have established within my heart. My search for safety, security, and stability was finally over. All I had known before I knew Him was chaos and confusion when it came to the relationships in my life, but I now had the assurance that with Him, I could know beyond a shadow of a doubt what to expect.

He was good.

He was kind.

He was faithful.

He was trustworthy.

He was for me.

He was LOVE.

Not the false impression of love that I had been offered along the way, but real love. Love that never fails or falters and isn't based on anything but who He claims to be.

And even better, I learned that, according to Hebrews 13:8, He is the same yesterday, today, and forever.

His love never changes.

His love isn't based on my behavior or His mood.

His love says what it means and means what it says.

This was the love I had been looking for my entire life.

Mathematician I am not, not even close, but even I could add up the equation that His Word offered to me. The more of God's Word I took in, the more I came to understand that He was a father like one I'd never known.

A decision had to be made. Either I was going to believe His Word was true, all of it, or I wasn't. All or nothing tendencies that I have, I couldn't pick and choose what to believe and what not to believe. I chose to allow His Word to be the authority in my life.

From that point forward and to this day, if my heart and His Word meet face to face with a conflict of interests, it's my heart that will have to bow down. Admittedly, sometimes it's a journey, a process, a knock-down, drag-out fight; in the end, however, every single time, I am the one who throws in the towel.

Without establishing the ultimate truth of His Word within my heart, I have no firm foundation on which to stand.

Chapter Twenty-Eight

> *Trust in the LORD with all your heart, and lean not on your own understanding; In all your ways acknowledge Him, and He shall direct your paths.*
>
> PROVERBS 3:5-6

I had been my own boss for a while and, frankly, was exhausted with trying to figure everything out on my own. My independence—masked as the freedom for which I had yearned—ended up being a burden when it came to the reality of living this life and making the decisions that would determine the course of my future.

Slowly, I began to exchange, "You're not the boss of me; don't tell me what to do" for, "Father, I need your wisdom, your guidance, and your discernment to navigate this walk... I can't do it without you." For one who despised the idea of being weak, to even admit that I needed Him was a struggle.

Those same authority issues that I had as a young adult followed me into my marriage.

It was the day of our ten-mile training run, and I was thankful to have the excuse of needing to meet with my training partner to get out of the house. My husband and I had had an intense "fellowship" that morning, and my still-simmering saltiness at him helped fuel my feet.

We had fought over which vehicle we were going to take somewhere. Neither of the choices was stellar. The minivan was on its last leg and had no AC. The station wagon wasn't in much better condition but used less gas to run. It was a season in our lives when money was tight, and every penny was counted. My husband wanted me to take the wagon. It made more sense to me to take the van. I had my reasons... he had his.

He told me what he thought. I rebutted.

He told me why he thought what he thought. I returned the favor.

He, a little louder and with frustration, restated his case. I stood firm in my resolve.

I knew I was right.

My idea made more sense.

I wasn't going to budge.

Don't tell me what to do; you're not the boss of me.

He, like so many times in the past, gave up and shut up.

In a defeated, much softer tone, he shared, "Ya know, Tanya, you always talk about wanting me to be the spiritual leader of our home, but you are never really willing to let me lead. It always has to be your way, no matter what the issue is. Any time we disagree about the way something should be done, you fight with me, and you always have to have it your way. It's always your way, or else."

As I ran that day, his rhetoric replayed in my mind. I started picking apart his words, finding the places I was sure he was wrong. And then, within, I heard the soft, gentle voice of my heavenly father.

"Daughter."

And with just that one word, conviction poured over me. He was right. I knew he was right. It *had* been that way for all the years of our marriage.

That very same struggle I'd had when I came to the place of trusting, yielding, and submitting to my Lord was a place I had yet to come to in my relationship with my husband.

How about you, Daughter of God; have you struggled in this place? Is independence more comfortable than dependence for you?

Many would answer "No," yet they get angry with themselves at their own insufficiency and their inability to get things done and make things happen all on their own. God is such a gentleman, and although His heart is to lead and guide His children, He doesn't intervene where He isn't invited.

It reminds me of my once-two-year-old who, in that season of chubby cheeks and wobble walking, adopted the mantra, "I do it myself." Yearning for independence, she endeavored to do everything alone, even things she couldn't quite manage. Believing that experience can sometimes be the very best teacher, I would stand by and watch her struggle. It wasn't until she came and asked for help—usually in frustrated tears—that I would step in and make the wrong things right. If I tried to intervene prior to her asking, she would resentfully reject my help.

Daughter of God, you have tried so many times on your own to...

~ Beat the struggle

~ Conquer the battle

~ Overcome the burden

~ Accomplish the task

The Psalmist tells us:

"Blessed be the LORD, because He has heard the voice of my supplication. The LORD is my strength and my shield; My heart trusts in Him, and I am helped; Therefore my heart exults, and with my song, I shall thank Him." (Psalm 28:6–7 NASB)

Being willing to pray for God to lead me was only the first step. I then had to trust that He would lead me, and know that where He led me was in my best interest. I began to slowly but surely unlearn the lesson of, "I do it myself."

This is what the LORD says:

"Cursed is the one who trusts in man,

Who draws strength from mere flesh

and whose heart turns away from the LORD.

That person will be like a bush in the wastelands;

They will not see prosperity when it comes.

They will dwell in the parched places of the desert,

In a salt land where no one lives.

But blessed is the one who trusts in the LORD,

Whose confidence is in him.

They will be like a tree planted by the water

That sends out its roots by the stream.

It does not fear when heat comes;

Its leaves are always green.

It has no worries in a year of drought

And never fails to bear fruit."

(Jeremiah 17:5–8 NIV)

God's Word is full of examples of not only His willingness but also His deep desire to lead His children. You see, Daughter of His, He already is sure of what we are still figuring out; that He knows what's best for us and will always lead us in that direction.

Daughter of God, begin to allow Him to lead you today.

PRAYER

Father, thank you that You lead me. Because You lead me, I can be confident that in whatever situation I'm in, You are right there with me, never leaving my side. When I ask, Lord, You are always faithful to give me Your wisdom, helping me to know how to move forward and what decisions to make.

YOU ARE LED
Questions for Journal & Discussion

1. Are you able to identify with any lies mentioned at the beginning of this section related to not being led by God? If so, what specific biblical truths have you learned that will help you to overcome that lie?

2. Are you able to identify a decision you have made that was motivated by something other than the wisdom and leading of God? Are you able to recognize God's redemption even when this has happened?

3. Are you able to identify a time when you have experienced peace that passes all understanding? If so, how did this gift of peace impact your ability to move forward?

4. Are you able to recognize areas where you have struggled with control issues? If so, how will you move forward from here?

5. Are you able to discern whether dependence or independence is more comfortable for you? Is your response determined by the various relationships within your life?

SECTION SIX
You Are Supplied

The Lord is my Shepherd; I shall not want.

PSALM 23:1

Chapter Twenty-Nine

> *For your Father knows the things you have*
> *need of before you ask Him.*
> MATTHEW 6:8

As a new believer and a young woman, I had so very many needs, and the people who were *supposed* to fill them simply couldn't. Many times, in this life, things don't happen the way they are *supposed* to or do happen that *aren't supposed* to.

I'm not alone in this; in both my office and my ministry, I meet women who have very real needs. With hearts of grief, they look at me through tears, seeing no remedy for their as-of-yet un-redeemed situation.

These daughters of God are devastated, disappointed, and in despair when those things in life that aren't supposed to happen do happen.

The young mother isn't *supposed* to be infertile.

The mother of young children isn't *supposed* to pass away.

The husband of many years isn't *supposed* to have an affair.

The young adult child isn't *supposed* to stray from the truth with which they were raised.

The beautiful newborn baby isn't *supposed* to die before they've had a chance to live.

The teenage daughter isn't *supposed* to be murdered.

The adult son isn't *supposed* to commit murder.

The beloved grandma isn't *supposed* to lose her memory.

One of the ways we can overcome these very difficult struggles—when the *supposed to*, for one reason or another, simply does not come to pass—is by knowing and trusting the truth of Philippians 4:19. Not only does your heavenly Father see you, but He also loves you, and His heart truly is to provide for every single one of your needs according to His riches in glory.

God wants our *supposed to's* to come to pass as well. The inner angst that passionately cries out, "It wasn't supposed to be this way!" mirrors the heart of our Heavenly Father. He, too, grieves the pain, loss, and suffering we experience as His children. Throughout the entirety of our struggle, He is actively anticipating the moment we will run boldly to His throne of grace and find help in our time of need (Hebrews 4:16).

Revelation 21:4 gives us a glimpse into the heart of God:

And God will wipe away every tear from their eyes; there shall be no more death, nor sorrow, nor crying. There shall be no more pain, for the former things have passed away.

This foreshadowing of heaven is how the Father originally intended life to be. It reflects life in the Garden of Eden before sin entered this world. It's what life would have looked like forever had that whole eating-the-fruit-God-said-not-to-eat incident not happened. But it did happen, and as a result, God's children live in the effects of a world infiltrated by sin.

And yet, ever the redeemer and restorer of our lives, our God valiantly cheers us on.

He encourages us to live our best life anyway.

He reminds us of who He is and who we are.

He supports us on every leg of this race.

Not the faraway, indifferent God that some believe He is, He assures us in His Word that He is acutely aware of our pain and desires to bring comfort.

The LORD is near to those who have a broken heart, and saves such as have a contrite spirit. (Psalm 34:18)

He heals the brokenhearted and binds up their wounds. (Psalm 147:3)

When what we experience does not align with what is good, the stark differences between life on this earth and our life in eternity come face to face.

For I know the plans I have for you," declares the LORD, "plans to prosper you and not to harm you, plans to give you hope and a future. (Jeremiah 29:11 NIV)

God is a good father who wants good things in our lives. Often, when women experience things that are not good in their life, they struggle with the "whys." In turn, they lay at the feet of our Heavenly Father the responsibility for all the horrible, painful, wretched things they have experienced.

Things He would *never* have chosen for them.

Things that *grieved* His heart as they were happening.

Things He *longs* to redeem.

The result is a difficulty in truly trusting Him, or trusting that He is good, which often leads to hearts reserved, a lip-service relationship with heart under lock and key. Women who go to church, do Bible studies, and serve in the nursery.

But, due to the painful events in their life, they determined deep down inside that the God who permitted or caused such bad things to happen must not be truly good, either.

Have you struggled to believe that your Heavenly Father is truly good?

Daughter of God, this is what I know. God is not the author of the bad things that happen in our lives.

> Every good gift and every perfect gift is from above, and comes down from the Father of lights, with whom there is no variation or shadow of turning. (James 1:17)

Isaiah 5:20 tells us to be careful not to call evil good and good, evil. It's important that we not attribute the horrible things that happen in people's lives to God's desire for them.

"God must be up to something really good to let this happen."

"Everything happens for a reason."

"You are going to have an amazingly powerful ministry because of this."

"God won't give you more than you can handle."

Here are the facts:

〰 *Bad things happen for a variety of reasons.*

〰 *We live in a fallen world and have human bodies.*

〰 *People misuse their free will.*

We have an enemy whose entire goal is to assault the truth of God's Word within.

Here's the truth. Our God is a Redeemer. And even before we experience those bad things, He has already determined a plan of redemption. Within that plan of redemption is His supernatural provision to fill in the gaps where we have needs. It's pre-planned provision to mend every broken place in our hearts and lives. In this way, He is able to take the most horrific, wretched, and ugly experiences and, in the miraculous way that He does, bring...

beauty from the broken,

glory from the ghastly,

miracle from the mess.

In order to receive this redemptive provision that He has for us, we must, despite what we experience in this life, believe that He is good and know that He is always working in our lives to heal, redeem, and restore any place that has been stolen from.

What is it that you need today, Daughter of God?

~ Courage

~ Peace

~ Joy

~ Comfort

~ Healing

~ Hope

~ Redemption

~ Provision

~ Restoration

Whatever it is, this is what I know. It may not come in the way that you think it should or wish it would, but you have a heavenly Father who knows you better than you know yourself and is always endeavoring to get to you exactly what you need.

He loves you, and His heart is for you.

In order to receive this promise into our lives, we must believe it to be true. Once the eyes of our hearts are opened to this truth, we see things in a different way than we have before. We come to understand that although what should have been cannot always be, our heavenly Father, in His amazing and beautiful way, can "fill in the gaps" to make our broken places whole and our crooked places straight.

Chapter Thirty

> *You will keep him in perfect peace, whose mind is stayed*
> *on You, because he trusts in You.*
>
> ISAIAH 26:3

I have a strong affection for greeting cards. Choosing them, sending them, receiving them—just *passing* by a Hallmark store sends warm fuzzies coursing through my veins. There is little that compares to the joy of finding that *just-right* card for someone you love. The one whom you know is going to smile and feel especially special upon opening and reading it. It's like a tangible hug, a material smile, a holdable memento of affirmation.

That being shared, I'm sure it comes as no surprise that I can easily spend many enjoyable hours just browsing the greeting card section at any store that has one. In fact, this has always been one of my favorite activities *except* around Mother's Day.

For many years, the weeks before Mother's Day only served as a reminder of what I *didn't* have and *always* wanted. The cards filled with descriptions of motherly love, followed with sentiments of thankfulness and appreciation, only served to taunt my wounded, angry, and bitter heart. I felt cheated in the worst way. The most generic of generic cards would be chosen, signed, and sent with a heavy heart; I felt as though I was only doing was I was supposed to do. My heart longed for what those cards described.

My mother died the Sunday before Mother's Day in 2008. It was several years before I was able to face and grieve her death. Doing so was one of the most difficult and painful experiences I have ever known.

Accepting her death meant that I would never have from her the mama love I had always longed for. There would be no healing or redemption of that relationship; all hope was lost. The story was finished, and there was no happy ending. I remember feeling vehemently betrayed by the Lord in this failure to produce what I believed I was due as His daughter. Since accepting Him as my Savior, I had seen redemption in so many places. But not in this one, not in the one that had mattered most to me. When I finally faced and accepted her death, I yielded to the great gamut of emotion that grief offers.

I grieved deeply what I didn't have, what I'd never had, and what I wouldn't have.

Grief is an interesting creature in that it waits for you. If you choose to set it on a shelf and not give it the attention it's due, it sits patiently, as long as needed, waiting to be contended with. When, however, you come face to face with that grief, it is as fresh and new as the day you encountered the loss. And I grieved.

I crawled up into the arms of my heavenly Father, and I grieved.

He held me tight and poured His comfort and love over me in the way that only He can. Although all of this happened in the spiritual, I could tangibly feel His peace that passes all understanding. It happens often in my time with Him. I enter into His presence with strong emotion... anger, frustration, hurt, disappointment. But after a significant time in His presence, it melts away and is replaced by peace. In His presence, I am...

Surrounded

Settled

Still

Regardless of the situation, He calms the storm raging in my heart. Faithfully. Every time. I shift my focus from the circumstances of life to Him:

His love for me,

His faithfulness to me,

His grace for me.

Peace comes, and it is in that place that He reminds me of what is true. When the noise in my soul has quieted, and I can hear His voice within. That my mother dying of a drug overdose was not part of His good and perfect plan for me. That, like any good daddy, He hurts for my hurt. That it's going to be okay.

I grieved the life that my mother had, that it had never been what she wanted it to be. I grieved the pain and difficulties she went through, only some of which I was there to witness firsthand.

I grieved the way I had treated her. Offering her hurt in my own hurt.

I wouldn't call her "Mom."

I didn't go to her funeral.

She died believing that I hated her.

I grieved.

It was in the very midst of that grief journey, however, that the Lord brought healing to my heart; His grace and mercy poured out to me gave me the ability to extend that same grace and mercy to my mother. Each of us, in our own way, doing the best we could with what we had and what we knew.

It was in that healing that a veil was lifted from my eyes. As I examined the content of both my life and my heart, I realized that although I did not have the relationship with my birth mother that I would have desired, the Lord had given me *many* mothers.

Along my journey, I could not deny that many beautiful women had taken the time to invest in the woman I have become.

A mother loves unconditionally.

I have experienced that unconditional love.

A mother guides, supports, and directs.

Many have done so for me.

A mother encourages, cheers, and dotes.

My heart fills as I recall those women.

A mother gently corrects and brings truth in love.

I'm so thankful for those women in my life.

A mother is a friend, one you can have fun with and be yourself.

I smile with the memories.

A mother lives by example.

I marvel at the women whose footsteps I am honored to follow.

A mother listens with a heart that hears.

So many have taken time to listen to me.

A mother sees through eyes of faith.

Being treated as a treasure instead of trash helped me to overcome.

Chapter Thirty-One

> *Oh, that men would give thanks to the LORD*
> *for His goodness, and for His wonderful works to the*
> *children of men! For He satisfies the longing soul, and*
> *fills the hungry soul with goodness.*
>
> PSALM 107:8-9

As I contemplated these truths, I realized that I had a choice. I could spend the rest of my life continuing to lament over what I had never had with my birth mother, or I could choose a heart of thankfulness for the many beautiful and amazing women the Lord had placed within my life to love me in the different ways that they had. Instead of finding all the things I desired in a Mama all wrapped up in one person, He had spread out the love among many, to be offered into my life in different ways and seasons.

Indeed, He *had* supplied all my need—*for a mother's love*—according to His riches in glory by Christ Jesus.

Recognizing this truth freed me to see the many ways the Lord had provided, in creative ways through other people, the different aspects of what I have needed throughout my life. Isn't it funny how the opening of one door can lead to the unlocking of so many others?

~ The encouraging fourth-grade teacher who took the time to make me feel special.

~ The kind seventh-grade coach who not only told me about Jesus but showed me His love.

~ The gentle counselor who, while working with the adolescent me that did not value herself, still treated me valuably.

~ The abundantly patient men and father figures who showed me that men really could be "good."

~ The obedient Christian mentors who were able to see through the ugly, raw trash of my dysfunction and walk beside me to unveil the treasure within.

~ The faithful husband who, unable to understand the deepest places of woundedness within me yet personally experiencing the pain of them for years, still loved and stood beside me regardless of the cost.

~ The compassionate children who loved me deeply and graciously as I did my best to be the mom I never had.

~ The loyal sister in Christ who has steadfastly walked beside me, supporting me and cheering me on as I endeavor to yield to the calling the Father has placed upon my life.

And these are just a few of the places I'm able to see God's abundant provision despite the things and people that were supposed to be there for me and simply couldn't or wouldn't.

It took a while to get here, and the journey was long.

How about you, Daughter of God? Are you able to recognize places where your heavenly Father has been faithful to provide for your needs in ways you could not have fathomed? Are you able to remember the moments when He placed a person or an experience in your life that so clearly showed you that He SAW you, and as a result, you responded to the very thing you needed, brought to you in a way that only He could manage?

Chapter Thirty-Two

> *And my God shall supply all your need according
> to His riches in glory by Christ Jesus.*
> **PHILIPPIANS 4:19**

I remember the beginning of God teaching me of His heart's desire to be the provider of my needs. You see, as one who was not provided for in all the ways I should have been, I determined that if my needs were going to be met, it had to be I that was going to meet them.

I became my own provider.

I became my own protector.

I became my own defender.

But as so often is the case, when we strive to be what we were never meant to be, the means we employ to do so are frequently less than the best.

Deprivation of love, acceptance, and approval led

me to be a seeker of those very things. I was desperate. Octopus, suck-the-life-right-out-of-you needy.

Deprivation of protection led me to be my own protector. I was defensive. Angry, hard, and shut-you-out-of-my-heart-and-life-in-a-moment protective.

Deprivation of my needs being met led me to be my own need provider. I was determined. Selfish. I would step on you and around you to make sure I would get mine.

This last trait reared its ugly head one night at the conclusion of a Wednesday night Bible study at a small church I was attending. After Bible study came sweet fellowship, accompanied by sweet treats. I had scoped out the sweets as we studied God's Word, and had my heart set on the one chocolate-covered chocolate doughnut amongst the less desirable—in my opinion—glazed and cake varieties.

In the middle of the prayer concluding the study, I gingerly got up, walked over to the table, and staked claim to my treasure. By the time everyone else had risen and was making their way to the treats, I was two bites in and feeling proud of myself for getting what was mine. I was taking care of myself, making sure no one else stole from me what I had decided was my own.

The next day, my kind mentor friend called me out with questions. "Why did you get up before the end of study last night and grab that doughnut?" Immediately defensive (remember, I was my own defender), I very bluntly let her know that there was only one chocolate doughnut, and I wanted it. If I didn't get it for myself, then someone else would have grabbed it, and then, well... I wouldn't have been able to. A look serving as an exclamation mark accompanied the last part of the sentence I'd offered. *Clearly,* she'd understand the dilemma I had faced.

Isn't it funny, the little places in our lives where the Lord chooses to reveal the content of our hearts to us to teach us big lessons? Like my friend, He asks questions to help expose the secrets of our own hearts.

"Where are you?" (Genesis 3:9)

"What is your name?" (Genesis 32:27)

"Who do you say that I am?" (Mark 8:29)

With tender mercy and powerful truth, my friend spoke very honestly to me about what the Lord had spoken to her concerning this situation. She believed it was His desire that I would begin to trust Him at a deeper level. That as long as I desired to be my own protector and provider, He would allow me to, but that truly that wasn't in my God-given job description.

My job was to be His daughter and allow Him to be my Father.

Allowing Him to be my Father in the ways she described meant purposely relinquishing my own ability to care for myself and instead, allow Him to do the job He had been waiting—and wanting—to do all along.

This was no easy choice. It required trust that He saw me, and in seeing me, He not only was aware of my needs but cared enough about me to meet them. When I couldn't fathom how He could meet them. When I knew I didn't deserve for Him to meet them. In His time and in His way, He would meet them. That is what He had promised to do, and good Daddies always keep their promises.

My very favorite story in the Bible about God being our Supplier is found in 2 Kings 4:1–7. We are introduced to a widow who really needs a break. Not only has her husband passed away, but she also is in debt up to her ears, and as a result, the people to whom she owes money are about to take her sons away to pay the debt. She goes to Elisha and reminds Him that both she and her husband were servants of the Lord.

Elisha asked her two questions: "What do you need?" and, "What do you have?"

This isn't the only time God used this tactic.

In Deuteronomy 29:5, God took the shoes and clothes the children of Israel had and made sure they lasted, never wearing out during that forty-year trek in the wilderness.

In 1 Samuel 17, God took the slingshot David had and made it effective enough to kill the giant.

In Matthew 14:19, He took the loaves and fishes that a little boy had and multiplied them to fill the need of the thousands.

In this widow's dilemma, God used what she had to help get her what she needed.

A jar of oil.

In fact, it was *all* she had.

As she examined the jar of oil that she had, it definitely didn't seem like enough.

Not enough to sustain her life.

Not enough to pay her debt.

Not enough to keep her children.

Elisha told her to go and collect as many vessels (jars) as she could find.

In verse 3, he states, "Go, borrow vessels from everywhere, from all your neighbors—empty vessels; do not just gather a few." He told her that once she had collected the vessels, she should come home, shut the door, and pour the oil from her jar into the vessels until they were full. She did so, and the oil only stopped flowing when the widow ran out of vessels to fill.

More than enough.

Once every vessel was filled, the oil ceased. As much as her need was in the emptiness of the vessels she had acquired, that was how much oil came forth—enough to fill all of the empty places until there were no empty places left.

Verse 7 states, "Then she came and told the man of God. And he said, 'Go, sell the oil and pay your debt; and you and your sons live on the rest.'"

Chapter Thirty-Three

*The LORD is close to the brokenhearted and
saves those who are crushed in spirit.*

PSALM 34:18 (NIV)

My friend Kim.

Authentic, funny, survivor.

Married young, the result of a fondness which developed in high school and continued to grow deeper and fuller as she and her husband, Larry, lived life together, building a home, a family, and a business.

Best friends, they loved being together no matter what they were doing. Celebrating their twentieth wedding anniversary, they looked back at all they had walked through, and treasured each memory. Looking forward, they relished those things to come. Growing old together, grandchildren and greats, grey hair and gratefulness.

Just two weeks later, there was a tragic car accident, one that took not only the life of Kim's husband but the life of her mother as well. One that placed two of her three sons and her father in the ICU. She was shocked, devastated, and scared.

She recalls walking down the corridor of the hospital, bearing the weight not only of her own grief but that of the entire community around her. Surrounded by others, she was unable to recall a time she felt more alone.

Managing to get through the double funeral, she was not yet able to contend with the depth of the loss through which she would have to navigate.

"No mom to get me through the loss of my husband."

"No husband to get me through the loss of my mom."

"No father to walk beside my three boys as we grieve together."

She was overwhelmed with not only the loss of those she loved so deeply but also with the loss of her own precious life as she had known it.

The life she was now living didn't feel like much of a life at all.

Life, as it so stubbornly does, refused to stop. Her eldest son was a senior in high school that year, but the tragedy overshadowed the plethora of momentous and celebratory senior events. He had been one of the drivers in the accident, so negative perceptions were formed, and public accusations were made that painted him as being responsible.

It was too much to bear; too much to bear alone.

At the state basketball tournament that year, rather than allowing her to revel in the moment, reporters relentlessly harassed Kim for information.

John noticed and came to the rescue.

John had been there all along, both before and after the accident. Larry's acquaintance and golf buddy, he became a source of tremendous support for the family that was left behind. Having known Larry, he grieved with the family and for the family at the profound loss they all had experienced.

Kim shares:

"We laughed together, and oh, we cried together for my husband, his friend, and us as a couple."

As time passed, slowly their fondness for one another grew stronger. Experiencing a common bond in their love for Larry—Kim as his wife and John as his friend—they both did all they could to help Kim and Larry's three sons move forward as best as possible.

Eventually, they married. And in those moments when Kim still grieves for the husband that she lost, John grieves with her, for her, and beside her.

Kim describes her now-husband John as a Godly man that loves her well. A wonderful stepfather to her boys, he has been faithful in being there for them when they needed him. She shares that he is exactly the man she needed in her life after Larry was with Jesus. Her heart is thankful for her new best friend.

In a miraculous and unexpected way, God took something Kim had in her life—her husband's friend—and provided something that she needed.

Chapter Thirty-Four

> *To give them beauty for ashes, the oil of joy for*
> *mourning, the garment of praise for a spirit of*
> *heaviness; that they may be called trees of righteousness,*
> *the planting of the* LORD, *that He may be glorified.*
> ISAIAH 61:3

Sometimes people in similar circumstances need different things.

Let me introduce you to my sister Amy. A sister not by birth, but of the heart—because, undoubtedly, we have the same Father.

Amy's husband passed away suddenly in 2016.

Suddenly, unexpectedly, and tragically.

They had been married for almost twenty-five years. They loved one another deeply. Terry's death was a huge shock and loss for all that knew him. His memorial service was filled with fond memories of the many that had been touched by his life and the way Jesus radiantly shined out of him with joy and exuberance. Wholehearted in all that he did, Terry no doubt ran full speed into the arms of his Savior when he stepped foot into eternity.

Amy and her fourteen year-old daughter, Samantha, were left behind.

It was a difficult season, to say the least. In a moment, Amy's entire identity and living arrangement changed. She was a grieving widow, a single mother, and living alone.

Amy and Terry were "snow birds," living in Wisconsin when it didn't resemble the frozen tundra and in Virginia when it did. Amy had friends that had become like family in both places. After Terry's home-going, as she contemplated her next steps, she had become fully convinced that it was His desire that she remain in Virginia. This didn't make sense when considering the size of the support system she had in Wisconsin compared to that which she had in Virginia, yet she knew that that was what her Father had said.

And so, she stayed. She grieved. She did her best to get up every single day and be the mother her daughter needed.

Amy and I did a ministry event together just four months after Terry died. It was a several-days event in which we poured into girls and young leaders. The second day of the event was Amy and Terry's twenty-fifth wedding anniversary.

It wasn't supposed to be this way.

Terry had always been Amy's number one support and encourager in all things in life and ministry. A crucial facet of the ministry that Amy and Terry walked in was the influence of a Godly male who provided support and encouragement to the young women to which they ministered. These women needed a man who could help fill in the practical gaps that may have been missed in their childhood. Through their encounter with a Spirit-led man, they learned relationship skills that would help them move forward in life, equipped to be successful and independent.

Cheerleader extraordinaire, Terry was the one who consistently nudged Amy to stretch beyond her comfort zone and walk in the places that God had called her, especially in this specific ministry event. It was a bittersweet day as she saw so many whose lives had been touched by Terry while, at the same time, so desperately missing him and his presence. In fact, when they realized that the ministry event schedule would conflict with their anniversary, it had been *his* decision to prioritize the weekend of ministry. "We can celebrate anytime, baby..."

I stood by and watched this woman of grace, strength, and courage work the event like a rock star, allowing Jesus to flow out of her in beautiful and amazing ways to impact the lives of so many. I was amazed by the Him in her.

The Lord called me to walk more closely by Amy's side. In fact, within a very short time, our two small clusters of loved ones, our family of four and her two, transposed into one family of six. Amy and Samantha needed a family.

God called us to be that family.

Amy needed someone to walk more closely beside her than a friend could. She needed a sister.

God called me to be that sister. Day to day, right by her side, face to face, and always there when she needed me.

And so this was the beautiful beginning of two small families, both living in a state where they had no other family, joining forces to become one family and doing life together.

God used the friends that Amy *had* to provide the family that she and Samantha *needed*.

Amy knew God had called her to stay in Virginia; at the time, however, she had no idea what God had in store. Similarly, at the time God called our four to become part of her family, we had no idea of the amazing and beautiful ways our own lives would be blessed and enriched by Amy and Samantha.

Amy and I are a ministry team, traveling and sharing God's truth across the nation as *My Father's Daughter*. Our gifts complement one another. Her gifts of planning and organization ensure that we get where we need to, when we need to, and with all the stuff we need to. More importantly, she is my right-hand woman. She prays with me and for me. Encourages me, sharpens me, and keeps me accountable. Her sweet and gentle spirit, combined with the discernment and wisdom of God in which she walks, are vital in helping each event to be most effective.

In ministry and in life, she is the sister that my heart has always longed for.

Since Amy has become my ministry partner, the impact of sharing the message of identity as a Daughter of God has spread farther and wider than it ever has before. I needed a ministry partner. I had prayed for a ministry partner. God provided that ministry partner.

God used the friend that I *had* to provide the ministry partner that I *needed*.

My husband, Luke, and I are recent empty nesters. The way things worked out, both our daughter and son left home to pursue further education within a month of one another. That is a huge change with little time to even ease into it! This was especially hard on Luke.

He always understood that being the father of our children was both a precious privilege and a high calling from the Lord, so he invested the majority of his time and energy into parenting them. Their absence in our lives, up-close and on a daily basis, left a gap in his long-time job description. Parenting adult children from far away requires a whole different set of skills. It's been an adjustment for sure.

Having Samantha in our lives has helped to provide a sweet uncle and niece relationship that fills each of their hearts.

God, through Luke, has provided a quiet, loving, affirming male support system to Samantha, who misses her daddy desperately. And Samantha has provided Luke with hugs, smiles, and playful teasing that helps to fill the gap of the absence of our children.

With the heart of a servant, Luke has always found joy in helping. He is tremendously blessed and fulfilled by the opportunity to help Amy and Samantha with things that are more suited to a male. He is the servant that serves as the head of this menagerie of hearts and lives as he intentionally submits his heart to the one whom he serves.

Luke, like Terry, is a strong supporter of the ministry to which Amy and I are called. He takes an active role in this ministry in every place he can. As chief cook, server, and cleaner-upper at My Father's Daughter women's retreats, he demonstrates through quiet service that men, indeed, can be good, kind, and selfless.

Each woman, young or old, that enters our home is offered a glimpse of Christ-centered manhood demonstrating to them affirmation and acceptance. Luke humbly, and with quiet strength, provides the presence of a male that is safe.

We are all thankful for one another and so aware of the very many ways our Heavenly Father took what we had in friendship and met our need for family. He not only met that need, but He also provided brothers and sisters in Christ with whom to walk beside, cheering each other on to accomplish more fully the calling that God has placed upon each of our lives.

Up to this point, Amy hasn't felt the need or desire to remarry. In this season, her greater need is for a sister and a family to journey through life with, and a ministry partner with whom she could run full force this race set before her.

> And my God shall supply all your need according to His riches in glory by Christ Jesus. (Philippians 4:19)

Daughter of God, begin to embrace the truth today that your Heavenly Father loves you and desires to provide for all of your needs right now.

PRAYER

Father, thank you that You are my provider. There isn't anything I need that You are not aware of. Thank you, Father, that at all times I can confidently trust that You will be faithful to fulfill Your promise to provide for me even when I cannot see or understand how You will do so. Thank you that You are a good Father in every way.

YOU ARE SUPPLIED
Questions for Journal & Discussion

1. What is the "supposed to" or "not supposed to" that you have experienced, Daughter of God? In what ways are you able to see the provision of your Heavenly Father in this place?

2. Have you ever or do you now question whether God is indeed good, based on something that has happened in your life? If so, what truths do you now possess that will challenge that lie in the future?

3. Are you able to think of a "More than enough" moment in your life, when the seemingly unredeemable was redeemed?

4. Can you think of a time when the Lord has used what you had to provide what you needed?

5. What need do you have today, Daughter of God, for which you can stand, believe, and trust your Heavenly Father to meet?

Epilogue

Beautiful Daughter of the King:

Many times, when reading a book that includes Scripture passages, I have been in such a hurry to *get through* the text that I have skimmed over or completely skipped those passages, being already familiar with the Bible story referenced or the verses being noted.

I want you to know that my words, in and of themselves, are worthless and have no ability to bring healing, wholeness, or life transformation. The only value that can be found in them is when the truth of God's Word validates them.

It is in knowing the Word of God that we are changed, healed, and set free.

And do not be conformed to this world, but be transformed by the renewing of your mind, that you may prove what is that good and acceptable and perfect will of God. (Romans 12:2)

It is in knowing the Word of God that we equip ourselves with the filter we need to strain every thought, enabling us to determine whether it is truth based on God's Word, or a lie.

It is in knowing the Word of God that we prepare ourselves to fight every spiritual battle well.

When we know what God has said, and it becomes the unshakeable foundation upon which we stand, the enemy of our soul is defeated in his desire to deceive us.

In the process of writing this book, I have worked diligently to be both thoughtful and intentional about including Scripture passages which help support what I've shared from God's powerful Word.

If you, like me in the past, have skipped or skimmed over those scriptural truths which have been shared, I would encourage you to go back and read them again. Write them down. Hide them in your heart.

It is in knowing God's Words of life and truth that your comfort, healing, and ultimate freedom are found.

Our Heavenly Father lets us know how important His Word is.

My son, give attention to my words;
Incline your ear to my sayings.

Do not let them depart from your eyes;
Keep them in the midst of your heart;
For they are life to those who find them,
And health to all their flesh. (Proverbs 4:20–22)

I have endeavored, in the pages of this book, to pour from my heart the critical truths about my Heavenly Father that have served as the foundation upon which I have been able to stand in my own arduous yet exhilarating journey from brokenness to wholeness.

It has been the process of learning what it really means to be His daughter that has enabled me to be healed and set free. It was learning, through His Word, who He is and who He says I am. Sometimes His hand reached down to pull me up, and sometimes He lifted me up from underneath, helping me climb out of the deep, dark hole where once I found myself. As a victim of severe and traumatic childhood abuse, I experienced neglect, rejection, and abandonment.

On this journey, I have come to understand that this same healing is the heart of the Father for every Daughter of the King. Those who recognize within themselves the ability to join the ranks of the least, the lonely, the left out, and the lost.

It's for those that have been victims as well of their own unique traumas and rejections, abuses, and abandonments.

My hope is that through reading these truths, perhaps in a different way than you ever have experienced before, the eyes and ears of your heart will be opened more fully to the deep, vast, and wide love that your Heavenly Father has for you.

That whatever you have faced or are currently facing, you have obtained a newfound confidence in the ability of your Heavenly Father to help you, as only He can, to walk as the overcomer He has called you to be.

To know that no matter what you have done or what has been done to you, His good plan for you remains, and as you continue to yield your heart and life to Him, He will be faithful to continue that very good work which He has begun in you.

To remember that nothing is too big or too hard for the one who longs for you to not only call Him "Daddy" but to know Him in just that way; as a good Father who *has* never and *will* never leave your side.

All for Him,
My Father's Daughter

www.myfathersdaughter.com